LIBRARY

Tel: 01244 375444 ~~F~~

This book is to be ~~r~~
last date ~~r~~

Race and Education

Studies in the
Postmodern Theory of Education

Joe L. Kincheloe and Shirley R. Steinberg
General Editors

Vol. 47

PETER LANG
New York • Washington, D.C./Baltimore
Bern • Frankfurt am Main • Berlin • Vienna • Paris

Alan Wieder

Race and Education

Narrative Essays, Oral Histories, and Documentary Photography

PETER LANG
New York • Washington, D.C./Baltimore
Bern • Frankfurt am Main • Berlin • Vienna • Paris

Library of Congress Cataloging-in-Publication Data

Wieder, Alan.
Race and education: narrative essays, oral histories, and documentary
photography/ Alan Wieder.
p. cm. — (Counterpoints; v. 47)
1. Discrimination in education—United States—History. 2. Afro-American—
Education—Social aspects—United States—History. 3. School integration—
United States—History. 4. Racism—United States—History. 5. United
States—Race relations. I. Title. II. Series: Counterpoints (New York, N.Y.);
vol. 47.
LC212.2.W53   379.2'6—dc21   96-44620
ISBN 0-8204-3690-9
ISSN 1058-1634

Die Deutsche Bibliothek-CIP-Einheitsaufnahme

Wieder, Alan.
Race and education: narrative essays, oral histories, and documentary
photography/ Alan Wieder. – New York; Washington, D.C./Baltimore; Bern;
Frankfurt am Main; Berlin; Vienna; Paris: Lang.
(Counterpoints; Vol. 47)
ISBN 0-8204-3690-9
NE: GT

Front Cover Photograph by Edwin Rosskam: "Boy in Front of Apartment
House, Chicago."

Cover design by Nona Reuter.

The paper in this book meets the guidelines for permanence and durability
of the Committee on Production Guidelines for Book Longevity
of the Council of Library Resources.

Printed in the United States of America.

To my folks, Seymour and Sally,
for their continuing love;
and to my sons, Nathan and Joel,
with hope that their children will know a less racist world

Contents

Acknowledgments

With a book like this, for which the writing began in the late seventies and ended in 1996, the author owes several debts. Colleagues and friends throughout the country have read my work and I thank them for their critical comments. I would also like to thank Shirley Steinberg and Joe Kincheloe for welcoming my book to their series. Their encouragement and positive spirit have made the book a reality.

My greatest debt during the New Orleans project, presented in Section Two, is to those people who welcomed me into their homes and offices and told me their stories: the Prevosts, Tates, Bridges, and Ettienes, as well as the Conners and Chandlers whose children were the only ones still attending the two integrated schools at the end of the school year. Jack Stewart, the principal of McDonogh 19 school, and two teachers, Les Scharfenstein and Josie Ritter, were particularly generous with their time.

Some of the white families who boycotted integrated schools also allowed me to interview them. Although I did not share their viewpoints, I found that like the Blacks who integrated and the whites who stayed, they were not identical and monolithic in their motivations or behavior. For instance, while one of my anonymous informants remained convinced twenty years after school integration that Blacks represented evil and school integration had destroyed the schools and country, a second white resister returned his children to the integrated school the next year and twenty years after integration was active in a community that had become predominantly Black.

Other informants deserve thanks. Betty Wisdom, Ann Dlugos, and Peggy Murchison were members of a white liberal group that nurtured school integration, and they each spent their time providing their recollections and reflections. Col-

Collectively, the people I interviewed taught me a great deal about school integration and race and education in the United States. They also reinforced my respect for the interview process by trusting me with their stories.

I took the photographs that appear in "Possibilities, Lost Possibilities, No Possibilities" throughout the country while the "South Carolina and Me" photographs come from South Carolina. Many of the faces are anonymous but I thank the people at the University of South Carolina Childcare Center, Children's Garden, the Columbia Jewish School, and Five Points School for allowing me to photograph the children in their care. I also am indebted to my colleague Craig Kridel, who has supported my photographic work and provided me with a venue for exhibitions at the University of South Carolina's Museum of Education. More than just a colleague, he is a good friend.

Finally, I thank Tom Berg of the University of Northern Iowa, David Angus of the University of Michigan, and Jeffry Mirel of Northern Illinois University. All three are friends more than colleagues and although we do not always agree on political issues, the spirit and humanity of our interaction is what is essential. Although none of these men is responsible for my work, each is part of it. I treasure their criticism, ideas, and, most importantly their friendship.

Permissions

Most of the essays in this book have been published previously, and I would thank the publishers and copyright holders for permission to republish them in this collection.

Chapter 1. Race and Education: A Review Essay
   Originally published under the same title in *Equity and Excellence* (December 1994).

Chapter 2. Robert Coles Reconsidered: A Critique of the Portrayal of Blacks as Culturally Deprived
   Originally published under the same title in *The Journal of Negro Education* (Fall 1981).

Chapter 3. Possibilities, Lost Possibilities, No Possibilities: Images of Middle Class Children and Lower Class Adults
   Originally published in *The International Journal of Qualitative Studies in Education* (1988).

Chapter 4. Visual Sociological Portrayals of Race and Childhood: Case Studies from the Thirties
   Originally published under the same title in *Multicultural Review* (Fall 1985).

Chapter 5. Common Ground: A Review of Reviews
   Originally published in *Educational Studies* (Winter 1986).

Chapter 6. The New Orleans School Crisis: Causes and Consequences
   Originally published under the same title in *Phylon* (Spring 1988).

Chapter 7. One Who Stayed: Margaret Conner and the New Orleans School Crisis

Originally published under the same title in *Louisiana History* (Spring 1985).

Chapter 8. One Who Left and One Who Stayed: Teacher Recollections of School Desegregation in New Orleans

Originally published under the same title in Altenbaugh, R. *The Teacher's Voice* (London: Falmer, 1991).

Chapter 9. The New Orleans School Crisis: The Blacks Who Integrated

Originally published under the same title in *Vitae Scholasticae* (1984/1985).

Chapter 11. The Brown Decision, Academic Freedom and White Resistance: Dean Chester Travelstead and the University of South Carolina

Originally published under the same title in *Equity and Excellence* (1995).

Chapter 13. Afrocentrisms: Capitalist, Democratic, and Liberationist Portraits

Originally published under the same title in *Educational Foundations* (Winter 1992).

Introduction

In the early 1950s as Bernie Mehl was finishing his doctoral work at the University of Illinois he received an offer at Hampton Institute, now Hampton University, in Virginia. Hampton Institute, a traditionally Black school, was famous with Tuskegee Institute as a representative vocational higher education institute for African-Americans. Some of Mehl's professors cautioned him to avoid the position. If he went to a traditionally Black school, they thought, he would be unable to move on to other more prestigious colleges. But Mehl went, and shortly thereafter, as the *Brown* decision reached the Supreme Court, other universities saw Bernie as an expert on African-American education solely because he taught at Hampton. Mehl took a position at Ohio State in the mid-fifties and for thirty years his classes and his scholarship there focused on race and education.

As Bernie Mehl's student in the mid-seventies, I found the realities of American racism and its relationship to education becoming a major emphasis of my doctoral studies. During that time the "culture of poverty" often defined Black people in the United States and cultural deprivation theory served to categorize and label Black children. I was working on my dissertation on the education of turn-of-the century Jewish immigrants when I had an occasion to spend time in the homes of African-American grade school children in Columbus, Ohio. It was the winter of 1976–77 and the city as well as the entire Midwest had been brought to a standstill by series of blizzards. The Columbus Public Schools instituted a program called "School Without Schools." Families volunteered their homes and students and teachers met so the system could meet the state-mandated minimum-school-day requirements without requiring summer school attendance. Meanwhile, our Ohio State

undergraduate teacher-education students also had to complete
their student teaching, and I had to supervise them. What I
observed in the homes I visited were some of the same Ameri-
can-dream stories I had found in my dissertation research. This
time, however, the stories were from African-American people
in the 1970s rather than turn-of-the century American Jews.

That single wintry experience formed the next twenty years
of my academic work. The white racism W.E.B. Dubois began
to expose in the early twentieth century—which was examined
further in the writings of Richard Wright, Ralph Ellison, and
James Baldwin, among others—was and still is very much an
American reality. The Supreme Court ruled for school integration in 1954 and Congress passed the Civil Rights Act of
1964, but white racism continues. Gunnar Myrdal warned us
of the intensity of our racism in the 1940s and Medgar Evers,
Malcolm X, Martin Luther King Jr., and many others, gave
their lives to the struggle for racial equality. But white racism
continues.

When I finished my doctoral studies in 1977 I considered
race and education America's most pressing issues. I see no
reason to revise that conclusion in 1997. The essays in this
collection represent the last twenty years of my academic work
and my stuggle to understand the relationship of white racism
and education in the United States. The sad reality is that the
issues that preceded the *Brown* decision, the Civil Rights Act,
and the civil rights movement, remain with us: racial inequality in our schools and society, and such overt examples of white
racism as the recent epidemic of African-American church
bombings. Accordingly, the ideas and issues addressed in these
essays on race and education, essays that span the last twenty
years, remain relevant as we look toward the twenty-first century.

This book presents three types of essays, each providing
different lenses through which one can study white racism and
education: narrative historical, sociological, and philosophi-
cal essays; oral histories; and documentary photographs. Each
reflects my efforts over the last twenty years to document the
relationship of race and education. The narrative essays revolve around issues like inequality, Sartre's conservative and
liberal bigotry, school integration, the culture of poverty, in-

school racism, racism in textbooks, and Afrocentrism. They are what Michael Frisch called "occasional essays," and each attempts to analyze issues consequential to the relationship of race and education. Narrative essays appear in all three sections of the text in the tradition of C. Wright Mills's "sociological imagination." Mills defined sociological understanding as a combination of historical, societal, and biographical perspectives. The narrative essays use this formula to describe and analyze race and education.

The oral histories in Section Two come from an extended project on school integration in New Orleans. I set out to record and analyze the recollections and reflections of the people involved at the two New Orleans schools that were integrated first. A group of people referred to as "the in-school participants" include the Blacks who integrated, the whites who stayed, the whites who left, teachers, administrators, the police, hecklers, and white liberals who nurtured school integration. Their personal stories are "grassroots" histories of school integration and they offer a unique perspective on the struggle for school integration as well as the broader issues of American race relations. Oral history features, of course, personal voices and furnishes an understanding that both enhances and humanizes traditional scholarship and official records.

Finally, the documentary photographs include portraits of race and education in the tradition of the Farm Security Administration work of photographers like Dorthea Lange, Walker Evans, and Russell Lee, as well as the more recent work of Milton Rogevin, Mary Ellen Mark, and my mentor, Bernie Mehl. One photo essay uses images from the thirties to show African-American life during the Depression. The other two photo essays are thematic and include my own photographs depicting current race relations. Like oral histories, these photo essays broaden one's perspective on the issues and themes that characterize race and education.

I have arranged this book in three sections. The first includes narrative essays on race and education, the first chapter being a recent essay on continuing segregation and racial inequality. The essay analyzes race and education in the United States currently and builds on Doug Massey's argument that continuing segregation is the most significant barrier to racial equality. The essay also analyzes various contemporary sources like Andrew Hacker's *Two Nations: Black and White, Separate, Hostile, Unequal*, Studs Terkel's *Race: How Blacks and Whites Think and Feel About the American Obsession*, Elijah Anderson's *Streetwise: Race, Class and Change in an American Community*, and Jonathan Kozol's *Savage Inequalities*.

I wrote the second chapter, "Robert Coles Reconsidered: A Critique of the Portrayal of Blacks as Culturally Deprived," in the late seventies. Coles's work is instructive because he was willing to challenge the culture-of-poverty theory, which was the ideological commonplace at the time. Coles encouraged African-Americans to tell their own stories, which often painted better portraits of the American dream than of a culture of poverty.

Chapter Three, "Visual Sociological Portrayals of Race and Childhood: Case Studies from the Thirties," examines photographic portraits of African-American life by way of a comparison of Richard Wright's *12 Million Black Voices* and Stella Gentry Sharpe's *Tobe*. Wright's book includes photographs that depict the hardships of African-American life, while *Tobe* includes visual portraits of the wholesomeness of Black rural life in North Carolina. The reality of white racism emerges against images of the investment African-Americans make in the American dream.

A photographic essay on social class and racial inequality follows. This essay borrows a technique that Bill Aron used when he published his work on Venice, California, which compared the elderly Jewish community with the youth street culture. Aron juxtaposed photographs of each group in pairings that illustrate both the contrasts and the similarities among the individuals and the two cultures he photographed. The same sort of comparison and contrast appears in this photo essay, "Possiblities, Lost Possibilities, No Possibilities: Images of Middle-Class Children and Lower-Class Adults." Photographs of white children and Black adults shown together illustrate the racial inequality still prevalent in the United States.

The last chapter in Section One presents a review of reviews. The chapter analyzes the reviews of the most important oral history of school integration in the United States, J. Anthony Lukas's book, *Common Ground*. The chapter also provides a bridge to Section Two, which includes oral histories of school integration.

Section Two presents essays on the school integration experience in New Orleans. It starts with a narrative essay on the causes of the problems and the racism that accompanied integration initiatives in the city. It also includes three oral histories centered on the people involved at the two integrated schools. Chapter Seven presents Margaret Conners' recollections and reflections of what has been called the "New Orleans school crisis." The Conners were one of only two white families who kept their children in a New Orleans integrated school. Mrs. Conners's story provides a model of what oral historians have referred to as "grassroots history."

Chapter Eight tells of two teachers at the integrated schools. One chose to leave the integrated school for a neighboring school district; the other remained at the integrated school. This is a story of contrasts without, however, unyielding ideology. It is a rare portrayal of school integration in the voices of teachers who were involved.

The last chapter in Section Two centers on the Black families whose children first integrated New Orleans schools in 1960. At the time, each of the girls was six years old. Their stories as well as those of their families offer important recollections and reflections on school integration. None of these Section Two stories are alike; each of the Black families who integrated—as well as the Conners, the teachers, and other people involved—offer different accounts of the same event. Each of the stories is part of the larger picture of school integration in New Orleans and the nation.

Section Three includes three recent essays on race and education. The first is a narrative analysis of school history textbook treatment of race in South Carolina. The essay traces the textbooks' portrayal of race, beginning with the early twentieth century books and concluding with the two texts currently in use. The essay is a microcosm of this entire collection because it illustrates changes in race relations while at the same time emphasizing the racism that persists.

Chapter Eleven is an essay on Dr. Chester Travelstead who was fired in 1955 as the dean of education at the University of South Carolina because he publicly supported the *Brown* decision. The essay traces the controversy with an analysis of media coverage as well as Dr. Travelstead's own voice. This compelling story fairly represents South Carolina education and much of the rest of the South at the time of *Brown* v *Topeka*.

The last chapter of Section Three is a photo essay entitled "South Carolina and Me: Children, Diversity, But Still Oppression." This essay follows the form of the photo essay in Section One, but it contrasts the diversity of children with a Ku Klux Klan store in South Carolina. Like the narrative essays and oral histories included in the collection, it illustrates the contradictions in the United States as race relations change but White racism continues.

Section Four offers a self-contained chapter entitled "Afrocentrisms: Capitalist, Democratic, and Liberationist Portraits." It examines the recent move toward Afrocentrism and the infusion of African and African-American content into school curricula. These movements have been severely criticized in both popular and academic journals, but this essay offers a positive analysis of three different Afrocentric perspectives. African-Americans are, of course, hardly monolithic, and this essay provides an apt conclusion because its portraits of capitalistic, democratic, and radical Afrocentric perspectives explain that Afrocentrisms are less theories of exclusion than theories of possibilities that promote racial equality.

The essays in this collection appeared between 1979 and 1996, and some uneven writing and contradictions naturally appear. I have chosen, however, to keep the editing to a minimum and made changes only where clarity or historical fact required it. The essays are arranged thematically rather than chronologically in an order designed to build the story of race and education. But no two people come to a text with the same purposes and perspectives. Each essay can stand alone, allowing readers to follow their own interests. The four sections begin with an introductory note that places the section's chapters within the contexts of both the times they were written and the present moment. Collectively, they describe and analyze the racism that continues to confront our society and our schools.

SECTION ONE

INTRODUCTORY NOTE

The essays in this section first appeared in three different decades but each continues to speak to racial issues in the late nineties. Combined, they address the saga of segregated schooling continuing in spite of a fifty-year legal history mandating integrated schools. They also illustrate the racial economic disparity in American society in the face of the fact that African-Americans believe in and strive for the American dream. My photographs shot throughout the eighties similarly depict continuing racial disparity while the photos from the thirties portray racism and disparity, but also middle-class African-American life. Together, the essays illustrate both the hopes of African-Americans and the racism they faced historically and continue to face today.

Chapter 1

Race and Education: A Review Essay

Douglas Massey and Nancy Denton's recent book *American Apartheid: Segregation and the Making of the Underclass* addresses historical and current segregated housing patterns in the United States. Massey and Denton summarize prevailing theories on the underclass ranging from those of Oscar Lewis to Charles Murray to William Julius Wilson. The authors conclude, however, that the continuing cause of the underclass is neighborhood segregation. This review essay extends Massey and Denton's thesis to school segregation, the argument being that school segregation not only continues as the cause of America's underclass but is also the cause of persistent white racism and racial tension. The discussion moves on to the costs of school segregation as tabulated in the work of Jonathan Kozol, Andrew Hacker, and Elijah Anderson. A third section discusses the racial tension and continuing white racism depicted in Studs Terkel's book *Race: How Blacks and Whites Think and Feel About the American Obsession*. It concludes by discussing the importance of a moral and structural reinvestment in school integration as we approach the Twenty-first century.

American Apartheid

Massey and Denton (1993) present the demographics of racial segregation in urban America. While they acknowledge the value of the 1968 Fair Housing Act, their statistics point to an acceleration of racial segregation in American cities since then. They begin with this bold statement: "Our research indicates that racial segregation is the principal structural feature of

American society responsible for the perpetuation of urban poverty and represents a primary cause of racial inequality in the United States"(p. viii).

Massey and Denton spend time telling readers what they already know about the special aspects of housing segregation for Black people in the United States. They recall the historical differences in mobility for ethnic groups other than Blacks and stress the need to study racial segregation: "Contemporary theorists of urban poverty do not see high levels of black-white segregation as particularly relevant to understanding the underclass or alleviating urban poverty" (p. 7).

The history of what Massey and Denton call "ghettoization" receives attention from both the historical and the sociological perspective in chapters entitled "The Construction of the Ghetto," "The Persistence of the Ghetto," "The Continuing Causes of the Ghetto," "The Creation of Underclass Communities" and "The Perpetuation of the Underclass." The authors use graphs and charts to present the isolation of African-Americans from the turn-of-the century until today. They point to greater levels of urban segregation in the 1970 census than in 1930 and to only slight changes between 1970 and 1990:

> [T]here is little in recent data to suggest that processes of racial segregation have moderated much since 1980, particularly in the North, where segregation remains high and virtually constant. Among the thirty areas we examined, eighteen had indices above seventy in 1990, seventeen experienced no significant change over the prior decade, and twenty-nine displayed 1990 indices that could be described as high according to conventional criteria. Given that these thirty areas contain sixty percent of all urban Blacks in the United States, we conclude that the ghetto remains very much a part of the urban Black experience. Racial segregation still constitutes a fundamental cleavage in American society (p. 223).

Massey and Denton present the ghetto and racial segregation as the causes of racial economic disparity, white racism and racial tension. Poverty, infant mortality, teenage pregnancy, drugs, violence, unemployment, and school failure are all part of what they call "hypersegregation." They also recall a history of legal restrictive housing covenants that excluded African-Americans from certain neighborhoods as well as present-day redlining wherein banks refuse to provide loans to African-Americans:

The effect of segregation on Black well-being is structural, not individual. Residential segregation lies beyond the ability of any individual to change; it constrains Black life chances irrespective of personal traits, individual motivations, or private achievements. For the past twenty years this fundamental fact has been swept under the rug by policymakers, scholars, and theorists of the urban underclass. Segregation is the missing link in prior attempts to understand the plight of the urban poor. As long as Blacks continue to be segregated in American cities, the United States cannot be called a race-blind society (pp. 2–3).

American Apartheid discusses education with sections on Black English, "acting white," and reviews of Ogbu (1978) and Crain and Mayer's (1978) work on race and academic achievement. Its conclusions on education link us to Kozol's comparative study of segregated urban schools and wealthy suburban schools. "It is not a self perpetuating 'culture of poverty' that retards Black educational progress," Massey and Denton conclude, "but a structurally created and sustained 'culture of segregation' that, however useful in adapting to the harsh realities of ghetto life, undermines socioeconomic progress in the wider society" (p. 169).

School Segregation

In *Savage Inequalities*, Jonathan Kozol addresses the "culture of school segregation." His book, a sad but moving travelogue, compares the extremes of urban and suburban education in the United States. He visited suburban Chicago's ultimate model school, New Trier High School, where only 1 percent of the students are Black and 93 percent go on to college, many of them to Ivy League schools. The student–teacher ratio is about 20 to 1 and the student-counselor ratio is 24 to 1. A full-time, 48-person custodial staff manicures the magnificent New Trier campus:

Courses in music, art and drama are so varied and abundant that students can virtually major in these subjects in addition to their academic programs. The modern and classical language department offers Latin (four years) and six other foreign languages. Elective courses include the literature of Nobel winners, aeronautics, criminal justice, and computer languages. In a senior literature class, students are reading Nietzsche, Darwin, Plato, Freud and Goethe. The school operates

Table 1
Public School Enrollments

	White	Black
Washington, D.C.	4.0%	91.4%
Newark	9.7%	63.9%
Chicago	12.4%	59.7%
Birmingham	13.0%	86.0%
Baltimore	18.6%	80.2%
New York	21.0%	38.0%
Boston	23.0%	48.0%
Kansas City	26.0%	68.0%
Milwaukee	32.0%	55.0%
Cincinnati	38.2%	60.7%
Columbus	51.0%	46.3%
Des Moines	82.0%	11.5%

a television station with a broadcast license from the FCC, which broadcasts on four channels to three counties (pp. 65–66).

This description starkly contrasts with schools serving predominantly Blacks or other shades of color. Andrew Hacker's 1992 study, *Two Nations: Black and White, Separate, Hostile, Unequal*, estimates that 63.3 percent of African-American children still attend segregated schools. The percentage is even greater in the urban ghettos that Massey and Denton describe and Kozol discusses. The numbers in Table 1 are from Hacker's book (p. 162).

The urban schools Kozol visited in East St. Louis and Chicago were from 95 to 99 percent African-American and they present quite a different picture from that of New Trier High School. Kozol describes schools and neighborhoods where taxi cab drivers refuse to stop and where police guard the school grounds inside and out. He tells of a woman offering him a ride near one of the schools he visited, explaining as she drove that no one should be walking these streets. At each of these schools he found both students and teachers with hopes and aspirations. On the other hand, he found conditions, directly related to the "culture of school segregation," that promoted hopelessness and horror:

> What seems unmistakable, but oddly enough, is rarely said in public settings nowadays, is that the nation, for all practice and intent, has turned its back upon the moral implications, if not yet the legal ramifications, of the *Brown* decision. The struggle being waged today, where there is any struggle being waged at all, is closer to the one that was addressed in 1896 in *Plessy v. Ferguson*, in which the Court accepted segregated institutions for Black people, stipulating only that they must be equal to those open to white people. The dual society, at least in public education, seems in general to be unquestioned (p. 4).

The schools Kozol presents in *Savage Inequalities* appear to ignore even the "equal" part of "separate but equal." He refers to East St. Louis as "America's Soweto" and describes schools often closed to students when raw sewage backs up into the bathrooms and lunchrooms. It is a town where major corporations, Monsanto and Pfizer, pollute the air but avoid taxation by incorporating their plants so they remain just outside the town limits. It is a school system rife with teacher and staff layoffs, where the student-teacher ratio is at best 35 to 1, and where students routinely learn from substitute teachers. Within this setting Kozol spoke with hard-working talented teachers as well as teachers resigned to failure. He observed a home economics class where the students just sat around talking, and the teacher informed him that "we do not work on Friday." He asked the same teacher if the class prepared the students for a job:

> "Not this class," she says. "The ones who move on to Advanced Home Ec. are given job instruction." When I ask her what jobs they are trained for, she says, "Fast food places-Burger King, McDonalds" (p. 27).

This passage contrasts with Irl Solomon, who has been described in the St. Louis newspapers as an exemplary history teacher, 30-year veteran who came to represent the reality of his neighborhood and school, which he saw as a story of poverty and high dropout rates, with a high incidence of student pregnancy:

> But our problems are severe. I don't even know where to begin. I have no materials with the exception of a single textbook given to each

child. If I bring in anything else—books or tapes or magazines—I pay
for it myself. . . . I have done without so much so long that, if I were
assigned to a suburban school, I'm not sure I'd recognize what they
are doing. We are utterly cut off (p. 29).

Students come to Mr. Solomon's class and they appreciate
his teaching. They told Kozol that despair is not the rule
throughout the school. But one advanced student explains that
there is no sense going to physics lab because there is no equipment. The auto mechanics class cannot operate because there
is no money to install the equipment they have, and the list
goes on. Although there is little money and many "non-work-
ing" teachers in America's ghetto schools, many others keep
up the fight:

> "Sometimes I get worried that I'm starting to burn out. Still, I hate to
> miss a day," Irv Solomon said. "The department frequently can't find
> a substitute to come here, and my kids don't like me to be absent" (p.
> 30).

Solomon's students know well the price they pay for attending school in East St. Louis. They told Kozol that they would
rather go to integrated schools, and one particular student,
Samantha, talked about the racism she experienced in a sub-
urb not far from East St. Louis:

> Fairview Heights is a mainly white community. A friend of mine and
> I went up there once to buy some books. We walked into the store.
> Everybody lookin' at us, you know, and somebody says, "What do you
> want?" And lookin' at each other like, "What are these Black girls
> doin' here in Fairview Heights?" I just said, "I want to buy a book!"
> It's like they're scared we're goin' to rob them. Take away a privilege
> that's theirs by rights. Well, that goes for school as well (pp. 30–31).

Samantha's experience is hardly unique and is most certainly
connected to the housing segregation Massey and Denton describe and the school segregation that erects a wall between
East St. Louis and Fairview Heights. Popular television shows
like *Cosby* have addressed this type of racism, as has the academic work of scholars like Henry Louis Gates and Cornel
West. West provides a poignant example in *Race Matters* (1993):

> Years ago, while driving from New York to teach at Williams College,
> I was stopped on fake charges of trafficking in cocaine. When I told
> the police officer I was a professor of religion, he replied, "Yeh, and
> I'm the Flying Nun. Let's go nigger!" (p. x).

Ironically Samantha's mother tried to transfer Samantha to Fairview Heights. But, as Samantha told Kozol, it did not work out and she philosophically explained it:

> "Well," she says, choosing her words with care, "the two things, race and money, go so close together—what's the difference? I live here, they live there, and they don't want me in their school" (p. 31).

A younger student Kozol met at an East St. Louis junior high school talked with other students about segregation and integration. Her mother was more successful than Samantha's mother and the child attended Fairview Heights for a short time, one of only a handful of Black children, hardly an example of integration:

> Only one other student in my class was Black. I was in the fifth grade, and at that age you don't understand the ugliness in people's hearts. They wouldn't play with me. I couldn't understand it. During recess I would stand there by myself beside the fence. Then one day I got a note: "Go back to Africa" (p. 35).

In the same conversation, a 14-year-old girl summed up the East St. Louis school reality with a great deal of irony. She described having to recite Martin Luther King's "I Have a Dream" speech every February during Black history month:

> We have a school in East St. Louis named for Dr. King. The school is full of sewer water and the doors are locked with chains. Every student in that school is Black. It's like a terrible joke on history (p. 35).

Kozol found an environment similar to East St. Louis when he visited Chicago and observed the segregated schools in North Lawndale where Martin Luther King lived when he campaigned for integrated neighborhoods in the city. Kozol described an "anti-neighborhood" that includes one bank, one supermarket, 48 lottery agents, and 99 bars and liquor stores. Gangs run rampant and, according to the 1980 census, almost 60 percent of North Lawndale's adults are unemployed. Kozol recalled a tour of the neighborhood with a local pastor:

> "Dr. King lived on this corner." There is no memorial. The city, I later learn, flattened the building after Dr. King moved out. A broken truck now occupies the place where Dr. King resided. From an open side door of the truck, a very old man is selling pizza slices. Next door is a store called Jumbo Liquors. A menacing group of teen-age

boys is standing on the corner of the lot where Dr. King lived with his family. "Kids like these will kill each other over nothing—for a warm-up jacket," says the pastor (p. 42).

Kozol decided that the segregated schools in North Lawndale represented compulsory inequity and pondered whether the 50 percent high school dropout rate might be a blessing for both teachers and students. He met defeated teachers just as he did in East St. Louis. An elementary teacher told him, "It's all a game. . . . Keep them in class for seven years and give them a diploma if they make it to eighth grade. They can't read, but give them the diploma. The parents don't know what's going on. They're satisfied" (p. 46).

He also met an elementary teacher named Corla Hawkins with a commitment to excellence. Kozol describes her colorful, lively classroom with parents volunteering and children reading and liking what they read. Ms. Hawkins spends time each Saturday tutoring her students' parents so that they can pass the GED. While Kozol considers it important to acknowledge people like Corla Hawkins, he warns that many more teachers in segregated urban schools are defeated and resigned to conditions. Ms. Hawkins talked to Kozol about her school:

> We have teachers who only bother to come in three days a week. One of these teachers comes in usually around nine-thirty. You ask her how she can expect the kids to care about their education if the teacher doesn't even come until nine-thirty. She answers you, "It makes no difference. Kids like these aren't going anywhere" (pp. 51–52).

In fact, the students Kozol observed and spoke with in Chicago appeared even less hopeful than those in East St. Louis. One group of students said they planned to attend college, but it was April and only one girl had applied—and she had yet to submit her grades or test scores. The same group spoke of recent events in Moscow and Berlin but could not locate Moscow in Russia or Berlin in Germany. A few identified Jesse Jackson as the mayor of New York.

> Listening to their guesses and observing their confusion, I am thinking of the students at New Trier High. These children live in truly separate worlds. What do they have in common? And yet the kids before me seem so innocent and spiritually clean and also—most of all—so vulnerable. It's as if they have been stripped of all the arma-

ment—the words, the reference points, the facts, the reasoning, the elemental weapons—that suburban children take for granted (pp. 71–72).

Kozol visited schools in other cities where he found "the culture of segregation" much like the culture he found in East St. Louis and Chicago. The price human beings continue to pay for school segregation includes low achievement and high dropout rates, which lead to poverty, unemployment, swollen welfare rolls, poor health, teenage pregnancy, and crime.

The Prices of Segregation

Referring with despair to four issues—teenage pregnancy, welfare, drugs, and crime—whites then use them to justify ongoing racism. Unfortunately, one seldom finds a reference to the "culture of segregation" as a major cause of these social problems, and few members of the majority treat them as prices paid for a segregated society. The work of Elijah Anderson, like that of Massey and Denton, describes, however, the costs of our segregated society. Anderson addresses the segregated reality without denying responsibility for African-Americans forced into urban ghettos. Most important, he points out that segregation and unequal schooling lead directly to teenage pregnancy, welfare, drugs, and crime.

One must recognize this connection as part of the "culture of segregation." The statistics (see Tables 2 and 3) Hacker presents in *Two Nations* (1992) as well as his assessment of teenage pregnancy are poignant and instructive.

A major problem in our time is that more and more Black infants are being born to mothers who are immature and poor. Compared with white women—most of whom are older and more comfortably off—Black women are twice as liable to have anemic conditions during their pregnancy, twice as liable to have had no prenatal care, and twice as liable to give birth to underweight babies. Twice as many of their children develop serious health problems, including asthma, deafness, retardation, and learning disabilities (Hacker, p. 78).

Elijah Anderson's ethnographic study *Streetwise* addresses Black teenage pregnancy narratively (1990). Anderson presents the views of both male and female African-American teenag-

Table 2
Teenaged Pregnancies, Abortions, and Births

	Black	White
Girls who have had sexual intercourse by age 15	68.6%	25.6%
Girls who have become pregnant by age 18	40%	20.5%
Pregnancies among 15-19 year olds that eventuate in births	51.2%	46.4%
Pregnancies among 15-19 year olds terminated by abortions	35.0%	40.3%
Unmarried mothers aged 15-19 who keep and raise their babies	99.3%	92.6%
Total births per 1,000 women who have never married (all ages)	1,020	127

Source: Hacker, 1992, p. 76.

Table 3
Out-Of-Wedlock Percentages: 11 American Groups

Black	66.0%
Puerto Rican	55.2%
Native Alaskan	43.6%
Native American	42.7%
Mexican	31.7%
Hawaiian	31.1%
Cuban	17.5%
White	16.1%
Filipino	10.4%
Japanese	6.5%
Chinese	3.8%

Source: Hacker, 1992, p. 84.

ers, and he analyzes a sexual reality, the foundation of which is the hopelessness of segregated life in urban America. He describes sex wars where the adolescent African-American male seeks social status in his conquests while the female hopes for a situation-comedy life with a husband and children: "The girls have a dream, the boys a desire. The girls dream of being carried off by a Prince Charming who will love them, provide for them, and give them a family. The boys often desire sex without commitment or babies without responsibility for them" (p. 113).

Anderson describes a reality where young men can rarely provide for wife and child even if they would like to. He describes young women who derive status from what he calls "the baby club:" a world where teenage mothers show off their babies in expensive clothing and relish the compliments. They stage "baby clothes and beauty contests" in a world that offers few economic and social possibilities.

Anderson's portrait of the Black teenage mother often gets ignored in the context of the costs of segregation or, when noticed leads to further white criticism of an African-American society whites equate to the welfare society. The stereotypical view of the welfare recipient is the young, promiscuous Black woman who has inherited the culture of poverty from her mother and grandmother. Interestingly, this portrait of the welfare recipient has emerged rather recently—say in the last twenty years: "However, the figures confirm the common view that most mothers on AFDC have had their children out of wedlock. This is a major change compared with earlier years. In 1973, the largest single welfare category used to be women who were separated or divorced; now it consists of mothers who have never been married" (Hacker, p. 86).

Although the number of Black welfare recipients is indeed high, discrepancies in some of the stereotypes exist. While 40.2 percent of AFDC recipients are Black, only 10 percent of these people have four or more children and less than a quarter have been on the welfare rolls more than five years. These figures defy the stereotypical view of "more babies for more welfare money" as well as a generational culture of poverty. The question, though, is why white America continues to use Blacks on welfare to place themselves on the moral high ground. Academics on the left, middle, and right—Black and white—all question welfare as it currently exists (see for example, Wilson, 1987; Katz, 1989; Murray, 1984). The problem is that white America uses the stereotypical welfare recipient to justify racism. They seldom stop to think that a high percentage of African-Americans on the welfare rolls reflects economic, political, and social hopelessness, one of the prices of the "culture of segregation":

> The manufacturing economy provided high-paying jobs and could provide training (low skilled) for people with little education and no entering skills. Furthermore, in today's economy even middle-class families require two incomes to live comfortably. Young people graduating from today's underfunded local schools often are not able to read, write, and compute at the level necessary to obtain high paying jobs. They then become employable only at the lowest levels of the service economy, which pay subsistence wages and offer little training, or must work in "fast food" establishments or similar jobs at wages below what such jobs pay in the suburbs. Members of the Northton community have not been able to make an effective adjustment to these economic changes. Thus idleness is widespread, numerous young women with children are on welfare, married couples are increasingly rare, and conventional role models are scarce (Anderson, p. 75).

This economic hopelessness, very much a part of the "culture of segregation," forms the foundation of the ghetto drug culture. Anderson describes a "culture and an economy" sprung from the desperation of urban ghetto life:

> With the massive introduction of drugs into Northton, both a drug culture and a drug economy have proliferated. The attendant financial opportunities and possibilities for "getting high" compete effectively for the minds, if not the hearts, of boys and girls. The roles of drug pusher, pimp, and (illegal) hustler have become more and more attractive. Street-smart people who operate in this underground economy are apparently able to obtain big money more easily and glamorously than their elders. . . . Because they appear successful, they become role models for still younger people. Members of the older generation, many of whom are not doing so well financially, find it hard to compete, and in frustration some accommodate the younger people (p. 77).

The classic media example of this culture was the infamous drug lord funeral in Oakland, California, where people lined ten deep to view the procession. Anderson describes male and female drug sellers and users, but he also interviewed African-Americans who live in segregated ghettos and fight against the drug culture and drug economy. Here, he analyzes the connection between drugs and senseless crime:

> In some ways this behavior is not so unlike what has come to be expected of more conventional drug addicts. One important difference is the new boldness with which pipers and zombies approach criminal activity: they seem to lack a sense of reality and of the immediate consequences of their behavior. In their agitated state, zombies do things even other drug addicts would think twice about and perhaps resist. For instance, they beg aggressively from passers-by, they are known to engage in hand-to-hand combat with the police, or they may break into a car or house in full view of others who might call the authorities (p. 88).

Drug-related crime as well as gang violence, of course, are real issues to be addressed, but one seldom hears that African-Americans—those who live in segregated urban ghettos as well as integrated suburbs—are usually the harshest critics of this behavior. Anderson presents examples of individual African-Americans as well as community groups working hard to attack the drug culture and drug economy and to rid the urban ghetto of its gangs. These initiatives go unremarked in discussions of the hopelessness and desperation of ghetto life. African-Americans do not, in general, deny the high percentages of Black crime:

> Such information as we have about crime can be calculated in several ways. The starting point is that Black Americans make up between 12 and 13 percent of the general population, depending on estimates of the census undercount. In virtually all spheres—offenders, victims, prisoners, and arrests by the police—the rates for Blacks are disproportionate to their share of the population. Thus Black men and women account for 47.0 percent of the individuals awaiting trial in local jails or serving short terms there. They also comprise 40.1 percent of the prisoners currently under sentence of death. And they make up 45.3 percent of the inmates in state and federal prisons. Overall, more than a million Black Americans are currently behind bars or could be returned there for violating probation or parole (Hacker, p. 180).

The crime these statistics characterize affects many facets of everyday life in America's urban ghettos. It connects directly to the drug culture as well as the high percentage of female-headed households. It is another regrettable aspect of the "culture of segregation" that remains an American reality. The four issues specified here—teenage pregnancy, welfare, drugs and crime—all represent elements of the late 20th-century urban ghetto. We articulate them as social problems but not as direct prices of the "culture of segregation" and segregated schools. If anything, we use them as rationales to justify the continuance of segregation and white racism. African-Americans both recognize these problems and understand that white racism thrives on their existence. The racial tension in the United States today is a direct result of white America's refusal to address its own racism and, thus, of its own support of racial segregation.

White Racism and Continuing Racial Tension

The acquittal of the Los Angeles police officers who beat motorist Rodney King and the ensuing riots brought to the forefront the continuing existence of racism and racial tensions in California and elsewhere in the United States. Increasing incidents of racial attacks on African-Americans have been documented by both the Southern Poverty Law Center and the NAACP. The murder of Yosef Hawkins by white youth in Bensonhurst was promptly matched by the killing in Crown Heights of an Hasidic Jew by Black Brooklynites. The point is that racial relations in the United States are every bit as volatile now as they were before the *Brown* decision and the Civil Rights Act and before the social ministry of Martin Luther King, Jr. Might it be that the systematic perpetuation of massive neighborhood and school segregation has exacerbated misunderstanding, mistrust and hatred?

In his 1992 book, *Race: How Blacks and Whites Think and Feel About the American Obsession*, Studs Terkel presents examples of racial tension and white racism by recording the voices of everyday Americans—both Black and white. An analysis of Terkel's informants reveals hatred fueled by superficial media treatment and experiential portraits of the four issues we discussed earlier: teenage pregnancy, welfare, drugs, and crime. We might add the recent resentment of affirmative action to the list. A young African-American woman spoke of the media image that forms white America's misconception of Black people:

> We usually see the young Black men in a gang. They can't talk. They
> have leather coats and are trying to conquer the world by being bad.
> What do you see first: A Black person killed by another Black person
> or killed a policeman or stabbed someone. Of course, you're going to
> be scared of Black people. You can't help but think they're all that
> way. That's not really what Black people are about (p. 7).

The issue, though, is a bit more complicated. Because segregation is the present reality, Black people and white people
simply do not know each other. Some place the blame on Presidents Reagan and Bush; others, like Gunnar Myrdal, sadly point
to white racism as America's perpetual disease. The African-
Americans Terkel interviewed are enlightening because they
continually return to the problem of whites not knowing Blacks
and Blacks not knowing whites. This estrangement is, of course,
a product of segregated neighborhoods and segregated schools.

A second young African-American spoke with both sadness
and anger about white racist views. Speaking of her father, she
said;

> My father is the kindest, sweetest man you ever wanted to know. . . .
> He's very dark-skinned. It infuriates me to think that some little white
> woman would get on the elevator with my father and assume, just by
> the color of his skin, that he's going to harm her, and clutch her purse
> tighter. To think that my father, who's worked hard all his life, put us
> through school, loves us, took care of us—to think that she would clutch
> her purse because he's there. The thought of it makes me so angry
> (p. 7).

Many of the white people Terkel interviewed would have
"clutched their purses" and many spoke in racist terms. One
man told him that "the stereotypes of African-Americans are
true. I seen 'em. They live like low-lifes. Don't like to work. Let
their homes run down" (p. 5). A 25-year-old man expressed a
similar viewpoint:

> I'm not as bad as the people I grew up with. They hate no matter what
> they see. You're a nigger and they don't like you. I'm not that way. I
> take everybody as I see them. But no one can tell me that the stereo-
> types they have about Blacks ain't true. They do act like people say
> they do. There's a lot of them don't act like that, good people, but
> there's more bad than good right now. They don't take care of their
> homes, let them run down. Don't like to work. They get married ten
> times. I'm not saying a large majority but a majority. Just from the
> neighborhoods I drive through every day on the way home. They look
> like shit. They live like low-lifes (p. 140).

Both of these men described Black people they work with as hard-working and decent, but each stressed that the majority of Black people were not. A woman Terkel first interviewed in 1965 described how she had become a racist. When interviewed originally she spoke of entertaining Black friends in her home and about living in a world where Blacks and whites work and live together. She spoke differently in 1990:

> I think I'm a changed person. I realize one of the big reasons is that I see only the bad. I do have wonderful occasions to see the good. I've got friends. I hate to say Black friends, because they're just friends. . . . But for the ten Black people that I know who are very sweet and very good, a pleasure for anybody to know, I've got a hundred that are just the opposite. Maybe that's what's weighing on me so much. Because the majority of them are not the decent types of person that I would like to meet (p. 43).

All three of the people quoted above, as well as many other people Terkel interviewed, described a white racism based at least partially on stereotypes of segregated urban ghetto life. Their views reflect media portraits as well as their own experiences in urban America. Although each interviewee makes a point of exempting the "good" Blacks, each is convinced that the majority of African-Americans fit the stereotypes. The issues presented here as the prices of segregation form the images Terkel's interviewees use to describe African-American life. They do not discuss these issues as promoters of segregation but rather as traits of African-Americans. Terkel interviewed African-Americans who also condemned this type of behavior:

> I get upset when I get on the el and a group of Black fellows or girls, they act completely wild. Like they never had anyone to talk to them, "Hey act like a lady, act like a man. Sit down, it's embarrassing." Then you look at yourself and say, "Well, I see white people think that, because what they normally see is the wrong image." But they don't think there's a flip side to every coin (p. 38).

"There's a flip side to every coin" loses its resonance if Black people and white people never know each other. Many of the white people Terkel interviewed would be surprised at the negative view of welfare many Blacks hold:

> When you start using food stamps, when you start living under the stigma of welfare, you begin to feel less than a human being. Children

feel it, too. They feel it because they can't have the clothes that their peers have or they can't do the things they want to do. Welfare tears down dreams (p. 66).

White racism persists in the United States because white America does not choose to see the "flip side." White America avoids acknowledging that the great number of Black people stuck in segregated ghettos are decent people who struggle, but are slowly losing their hopes and dreams. This hopelessness in the segregated ghetto has precipitated the issues white Americans point to as the low road Black Americans take. The truth, though, is that most African-Americans still struggle, remain hopeful, and continue to believe in the "American dream." White Americans who live with Black Americans and truly cherish a multicultural society see the "flip side" clearly. In fact, the "flip side" is for them more the reality than teenage pregnancy, welfare, drugs and crime:

> I've spent all my life being scared to death of what would happen when the coloreds moved in. Some of my neighbors moved out when the first Black family moved in. My Black neighbors are a lot better than a lot of my white neighbors ever were. They care about their kids, they care about their property, and they care about me as their neighbor (p. 131).

This view came out of involvement and from learning to know the individuals in a community. Another white interviewee described his experience:

> We've been invited to their weddings and graduations. You go down the street, teenagers, anyone, you smile at them, act decent toward them, they give you back what you give them. It's an exchange between two equals. My old friends say, "How can you stay there? Aren't you afraid?" They rationalize, have to defend what they did. They can't say, "I moved because I'm a white racist." They have to say, "I moved because the neighborhood is so terrible." There are incidents here. We've had our car stolen. We got it back. The garage has been broken into. But it happened when it was a white neighborhood. But if you're a racist, you use that as an excuse to hang your fears on (p. 112).

Integration as a Moral Imperative

The two people who declined to escape Black people and remained in their neighborhoods express rarer and rarer views.

The United States remains a segregated society with its children attending segregated schools. The Supreme Court ruled for integrated schooling some forty-two years ago and we still remain a nation where Black people and white people remain apart. White racism sustains this "culture of segregation" and feeds off of the horrors the segregated ghetto produces—or, more accurately, white racism itself produces. People in urban ghettos trying to live the American dream, so poignantly portrayed in the work of Robert Coles and others, rarely appear in the popular media pictures. Thus, we create segregation which leads to poverty which leads to horror and then we cite the horror to justify our own fears and hatred: a vicious cycle that produces more and more segregation.

But Black people now tire of their wait for integration and seriously question whether white America will ever allow it to occur. Many African-Americans now side with Louis Farrakhan or push for Afrocentric curricula in the schools or send their children to all-male African-American academies or to private secular or Christian Black schools. Many of these African-Americans who now choose separation were once in the vanguard of the civil rights movement, integrationists who grew disenchanted with what they view as an impossible battle:

> We went out for integration and it hasn't happened. We put our eggs in that basket and they're cracked. You can march, you can shout, you can do anything you want to, but I think we have to cast down the buckets where we are. I did really believe there would be a harmonious getting along. I was all for Dr. King's March on Washington in 63. But I wouldn't take part in that now (Terkel, p. 139).

Such uplifting examples as the teachers Corla Hawkins and Irl Solomon and some of the students Jonathan Kozol interviewed who work hard in school and hope for integrated schools and neighborhoods seldom appear in the media as major influences on African-American life. The examples Studs Terkel provides of Blacks and whites living together and relating as human beings as well as the instances of comfortable school and neighborhood integration also seldom reach the public eye.

Some Black people call for separation as an alternative to the segregation they still suffer. This is happening at precisely the time when Black and white people need to get to know each other and live civilly and decently together. The need to live civilly and decently—the first in terms of human relations and the latter in terms of material comfort—requires integration. Moreover, Black and white people coming together has to begin with schoolchildren. If Black and white Americans are ever to come together as equals it must grow from a trust and understanding developed among the youth. Kenneth Clark, a scholar and key advisor in the *Brown* decision, reflected sadly on this continuing need:

> In the 1940s, my wife and I conducted experiments among little Black children. They found white dolls more attractive than Black dolls. If we had really desegregated the schools and increased the educational opportunities for Black and white children, if we had reduced the stereotypes, we educators could have changed those results. But we haven't and we don't intend to (Terkel, p. 337).

Professor Clark's resignation is shared by many who live both inside and outside of the "culture of segregation." Success stories are miraculous considering urban ghetto barriers. Lerone Bennett Jr., the executive editor of *Ebony*, explained for Studs Terkel his view of American integration:

> Integration has never been tried in this country. It has not even been defined. What is integration? If you put two, three Blacks in an all-white institution, it's not integrated. It requires a complete change in the way you think as an institution. Real integration involves a change in values (p. 380).

Real integration requires people to come together as human beings. For the East St. Louises of the world to disappear, people have to meet, know and care about other human beings. They have to live with each other and celebrate and suffer their similarities and differences. Integration means coming together; segregation means staying apart. Thus, we must bring children together at young ages so they can grow up together and bring our society together, civilly and decently and united. Only through school integration can Dick Gregory's reference to "the yet-to-be United States of America" ever transform into the United States of America.

Chapter 2

Robert Coles Reconsidered:
A Critique of the Portrayal of Blacks
as Culturally Deprived

In the early pages of *The Autobiography of Malcolm X*, Malcolm recalls a friendly teacher who told him matter-of-factly that becoming a lawyer is "no realistic goal for a nigger" (Haley, p. 36). Educators often cite this passage to illustrate the ill-effects teachers can have on minority children. But despite this lesson and despite the applause for books like *Pygmalion in the Classroom*, teacher educators, public school teachers, or teachers in training rarely question the culture-of-poverty thesis or the educational theory of cultural deprivation. Although appalled by the words of Malcolm's teacher, educators seldom discuss the Puritan work ethic or middle-class goals of a young Malcolm. As readers move through his early childhood to the admonition just cited, we learn that his father has been killed by whites and that his mother is in a mental institution. The situation certainly appears to be prime culture of poverty material, but when we look below the surface we find aspirations and educational accomplishments that are right out of the middle class.

Many representations of Black life in America are either false or misleading. They are also dangerous because they are taken so frequently as gospel by educators and others in the "helping professions." The three most popular interpretations are that Blacks live in a culture of poverty, are culturally deprived, and are socially pathological. Daniel Patrick Moynihan's Black matriarchal family, disadvantaged children, and multi-generational unemployment are examples of each, and a chronic lack of money remains a familiar theme.

These theories, swollen with ideology, are espoused by professionals who profit far more from their acceptance than do the Blacks whose welfare they purport to assist. The middle-class mentality so evident in Malcolm X is generally disregarded by the theorists, but this mentality is very much part of the Black American ethos.

An analysis of this mentality is found in the work of Robert Coles. His *Children of Crisis* series, as well as numerous articles, contain interviews Coles collected during the 1960s in which both Blacks and whites discuss their relationships in a racist but changing world. Children, adults, workers, housewives, the unemployed, the underemployed, civil rights workers, Ku Klux Klan members, doctors, policemen, and teachers are among those interviewed.

Coles's work remains exceptional, partially because of the irony and partially for the progression in his thought. When Coles began the interviews he was looking for pathology. He expected to demonstrate the depth of social pathology that our society allows to exist amid growth and progress. The irony is that he also found great strength, middle-class aspirations, and hard work. Next to resignation was striving and next to desperation were middle-class goals. Coles's people parallel the 56 percent of poor Black people and 58 percent of middle-class Black people who insist that America is still the "land of opportunity."

Who are these people? They are adults and children. They are workers and unemployed. They are the impoverished and the middle-class. And finally, in spite of these differences, they are Black Americans who have faith in public schools and believe in the American Dream.

Businessmen, workers, teachers, and parents speak of their own aspirations and values as well as those they hold for their children. In coastal Carolina, Beaufort County in particular, Coles describes a world of old stale bread and grits as the dally meal, a world where the diseases included rickets, scurvy, beriberi, and pellagra, a world where two-thirds of the people were ill-fed, ill-housed, and ill-clothed. Beaufort County is also the home of Hilton Head Island, host to the rich of the East and the Professional Golfer's Association. Somewhere between

the poverty and the resort lies "Hilton Head Fishing Cooperative, Inc." Cooperative members are Black men who understand the reality of Beaufort County and work to make a go of
it in spite of their knowledge of how the county limits them:

> A few of us, we figured we'd stay. We figured we'd build a few shrimp
> boats and try to get together; you know, work side by side and pitch
> in for one another. Then we heard we might get some help from the
> government, an FHA loan, so we could build a dock and a little rail-
> way to unload in, and carry the fish, and a place to work and store the
> fish we catch (Coles, 1972, p. 92).

Coles went on to describe the operation and finishes by talking about the cooperative members. Vital, confident, proud,
and industrious are the adjectives he uses to describe them.
The same adjectives describe a hard-working cab driver in
Cleveland, Ohio. The cab driver, Ray Phillips, tells Coles about
his family, his job, and about being a Black man in the the
United States:

> Everyone is looking at the Black man today and saying: who is he, and
> what's on his mind? I know. I flip from one station to another, or I'll
> meet a real honest fare and he'll say to me: Come on, level with me
> and tell me what you think of all our race problems. Well, I do tell
> him, even if he's a big, fat white businessman. I say: Mister, I'm a
> citizen of this country, just like you. I was over in the Pacific, fighting
> to beat Japan and win. I was under MacArthur. I've seen other parts
> of the world, and I'm glad to be living right here (Coles, 1967,
> p. 169).

Coles heard "glad to be right here" at least as often as he heard
"racist America" or the stoical, "this is my place, poverty." Ray
Phillips also told Dr. Coles, "If white people would only get off
our backs and leave us alone we'd be the best citizens this country has" (p. 169).

An equally patriotic and thoroughly Puritan work ethic point
of view came from a northern factory worker. Notice the dis-
dain for those who speak of the culture of poverty:

> I'm thirty-seven years old. I am called a Black man. The fact is, mister
> I work in a factory, and I have a wife and three children and we live in
> an apartment. I used to think there were a lot of people like me, thou-
> sands and thousands of them. I used to think I'm a worker, and there
> are a lot of workers like me at the plant, and some happen to be Ne-
> groes and some happen to be white, but we'd all been there for years

and we knew each other, and when you come right down to it, we're not that different. We spend the days the same way, and when we talk about what we do in the evening and on weekends, it comes out sounding the same then, too. But these days I'm supposed to believe I'm an oddball, a rare bird, you know. I'm supposed to believe I live in a ghetto, and all around me are these diseased people. . . .

Why don't people talk about someone like me? Why don't they call me an American citizen, not a Black man or Negro or all the other words? I am not out to tear society apart. I get up every day and go to work and come home and I'm not on heroin, and I'm not drunk, and my kids aren't experimenting with drugs and on the way to being pimps and prostitutes.

You know, it's insulting the way people try to create an image of the Negro as some pathetic creature who can't for the life of him take care of himself and has nothing he can really believe in and be proud of (Coles, 1967, pp. 200–201).

This man was neither resigned nor docile. His impatience with the portrayal of Blacks as "culturally deprived" and his anger are both serious and moving.

The comments of many of those Coles interviewed bring to mind Eugene Genovese's study on slavery, *Roll Jordan Roll* (1974). Like the factory worker just cited, Genovese takes issue with those who distort Black reality. His focus, though, differed. Genovese revised Stanley Elkins's *Slavery* (1968), which for a long time served as the final word on the American slave. Elkins's slave was both docile and resigned. What master said was reality and law. Slaves neither questioned nor acted, they simply did their work. *Roll Jordan Roll* documents the slave reality as something quite different. The history of Black Americans was rather one of working at freedom, reading and writing and demonstrating creativity. Genovese's slave and Coles's worker do not fit the popular portrayals of Black America. Both provide evidence of intelligence and vitality to which much of white America is still blind.

An excellent modern example of Genovese's thesis appears in the opening moments of the documentary film, *Strike City*. The words are spoken by a Black Mississippi sharecropper: "The reason we went on strike, I was tired of working for six dollars a day and was tired of my wife and kids working for three dollars a day" (Coles, 1972, p. 60). This man and other sharecroppers went on strike, let the fields rot, and eventually left Mississippi to find work elsewhere. Certainly they do not fit the sharecropper stereotype of resignation to a life of lord and

serf. Nor do they fit the description of apathetic Blacks provided in many of the current distorted views of ghetto life.
The kind of strength in evidence here appeared in Coles's
description of Black parents in Boston who in 1964 "vowed to
go all over Boston until they found 'a school better than a
prison, a school where the kids aren't without desks and sit-
ting all over the place and being told to shut up, shut up all
day long'" (Coles, 1967, pp. 30–31).

It is time now to turn to the teachers and parents of the
Children of Crisis. They speak of their lives and of the hopes
and dreams they hold for themselves and their children. They
also talk of current accomplishments as the embryonic stage
of those hopes and dreams.

Coles interviewed two teachers, Miss Simpson and Miss
Jones. We learn that Miss Simpson was the ideal of a young
and gifted high school student. Her reign as the perfect high
schooler ended, however, when she gave birth to a daughter in
her senior year. With her mother's help Miss Simpson finished
school. Her baby, retarded and sickly from birth, died in childhood. Two months after the child's death, Miss Simpson's
mother died, leaving her without immediate family. Shortly
thereafter, she received her college degree in teacher education:

> I think I started becoming a teacher when I was in the fourth or fifth
> grade. I did very good work, and the teacher asked me to help her
> with the slower children. I was very honored, and studied even harder
> at home to make sure I would be able to equal the teacher and keep
> on working for her. My mother wanted so very much for me to go to
> college and be a teacher. I think it became the one ambition of her
> life, that I not do what she was doing, that I become a leader, a teacher
> (Coles, 1964, p. 162).

Coles's discussion of Miss Simpson recalls the "American
dream" and the educational faith story of Leonard Covello
(1958). Italian immigrant, New York City teacher, principal and
area superintendent, Covello's commitment was continually
to extend the educational and occupational opportunities
for new groups of Americans. One finishes the *Children of
Crisis* section on Miss Simpson with a feeling of the same
commitment.

Coles's second teacher, Miss Jones, is a second-generation
educator. She tells Coles that her students:

. . . listen, they learn. They are not the children she sometimes reads about when she comes across an article about the ghetto. They are not beaten down or indifferent or wild. Certainly she sees her fair share of troubled children from broken homes, from homes as needy and wanting and hard pressed as any in America. . . . A lot of well-meaning and kind and sensible people in her opinion get the wrong impression: 'Those people talk about our children as if they're all retarded, or in rags, or unable to read or write. Those people picture them as troublemakers, as noisy and disrespectful and poorly behaved all around. I wish they would come to my school. I wish they could meet some of the children I teach—and they are from poor homes as well as solid backgrounds. I used to teach in an all-white school, located in a well-to-do section of this city. I had problems there, plenty of them (Coles, 1967, p. 81).

Miss Jones's opinion of her students juxtaposed with the accomplishments, goals, dreams, and values of Black businessmen and workers, offers an alternative portrayal of our society. Black Americans retell white Americans what America represents. Martin Luther King, Jr., it should be recalled, urged the movement to keep reminding white Christians that they were, in fact, Christians.

Another reminder of the American dream and the Horatio Alger story comes from the parents of the *Children of Crisis*. Coles described the father of an elementary school child, Tessie, who was one of three Black children who integrated the New Orleans schools and is one of the people we discuss in Section Two. Coles's description of the father depicts anything but cultural deprivation:

He is a college graduate. He speaks excellent English. He reads widely in magazines and paperbacks, particularly on world affairs and recent history. He works in the post office, sorting letters all day. His mother said that he wanted to be a lawyer, but getting him through college taxed her to the point of exhaustion. 'There wasn't any more money in those days' (Coles, 1964, p. 89).

One aspect of the culture-of-poverty home is the lack of books. How can a child be expected to read, one wonders, when he or she never sees a book? The truth is this question is rooted more in myth than in the reality of most Black homes. Tessie's home, for example, did not lack reading materials. She was not without attention, another culture-of-poverty family trait attributed to Blacks. Tessie's mother, father, and grandmother were all integral parts of her life. Her parents, like many other young Blacks, chose to have as little to do with the white world as possible. Tessie's grandmother had always worked for whites, and James, Tessie's father, viewed the practice as a continuation of the master-slave relationship. He was, in fact, quite an unlikely choice to let his daughter integrate a southern school system, until one hears his analysis of modern America:

> My mom still wants us to know what's going on in the white world, but a lot of us younger Negroes didn't much care for a long time. Then the Supreme Court decision came, and we realized we had to come out from our shells, and once and for all fight our way into the white world. It was a good thing people like her were there to help us. You need to know the people you're trying to get with (Coles, 1964, p. 90).

In Coles's work education continually appears as a path to success. Arthur, a third-grader in Boston, tells Coles that he has to work extra hard because "learning doesn't come easy." Coles then interviewed Arthur's teacher:

> The teacher does say he is improving. She says that Arthur continues to be taciturn, suspicious and slow, but actually has been learning quite a lot and has about caught up with "the national average in reading." The teacher adds a few interesting details. "The other day he said he was glad we 'changed things around' and mixed races and class here. He said he's made a few friends, a few white friends, and he's found out 'they're not any smarter than me. They're just better trained, that's all.' Arthur also told me a few weeks ago that he used to think he wanted to be a boxer, or a baseball star, or a marine guerilla fighter in Vietnam, but now he wouldn't mind being a lawyer. He said Negroes need lawyers" (Coles, 1967, p. 503).

The teacher's last observation is most interesting in light of former "student athletes" now suing their college for the basic education they never received. In 1980, one Black ex-college football star interviewed on the National Public Radio show "All Things Considered" said he had completed two years of college before an injury ended his career. He then flunked out of school without the ability to read, write, add, or subtract. His story has a happy ending. He felt embarrassed when he could not read to his four-year-old son, had learned how to read and write, and would soon be ready to re-enter college.

He laughed when he was reminded he already had two years of credit.

Coles also talked with Henry T. Rollins, a janitor and father of five. Rollins works two jobs to provide for his family, and his wants are modest: three good meals a day for his family of seven, warm clothing, a safe and clean house, and a high-school and ideally a college education for his children. For Coles, Henry T. Rollins became a philosopher of the American dream:

> I can honestly say [to my children]: I got this far, now you go and do the same, and do more, and go even further. That was something else my grandaddy used to say. He'd say: I'm walking down the road as far as I can, and your daddy, he's walking along, and he'll get farther along than me, and you, I'll be hoping you go farther along than both of us. I tell that to my kids. I tell them they've got to keep walking and it won't be long before they're way out ahead of me; and their mother and I, we'll be pleased to be looking at them, out there in front of us (Coles, 1967, p. 166).

"Out there in front of us" amounts to a continuing theme for many of the people Coles and Terkel and others interviewed. This is not to imply that they have completed their lives. It does mean that they envision greater possibilities for their children. Many of their households are strict almost to a fault. The Puritans would be proud of them. Their children live on schedules. They are clean, well fed, and polite. Their homework is checked by their parents. They are taught that schools and teachers are the means to a better world.

There is no doubt that the above is not always the case, a point acknowledged by Coles himself. Yet the middle-class mentality described here is at least as much a reality as the existence of "cultural deprivation." White America refuses, however, to give it credence. One wonders if whites might create the culture of poverty if it did not exist. My university students came to me disappointed because the people they tutored in the small nearby ghetto lived in neat homes, were sober, and were polite to their visitors and to each other. The tutors were annoyed with me; they wanted to help people who were really in need! Possibly the whole issue is summed up best by a Mississippi Delta sharecropper:

> The people who help us, we're grateful to them, but I wish they wouldn't keep on telling us how sorry they are for us, how bad we

have it. And I wish their eyes wouldn't pop out every time they stay with us and see we're not crying all day long and running wild or something. The other day a white fellow, he said how wonderful my home is, and how good we eat and get along together, and how impressed he was by it all. And I was sure glad, but I wanted to take him aside and say, ain't you nice, but don't be giving us that kind of compliment because it shows on you what you don't know about us (Coles, 1972, p. 89).

In the main, this discussion affirms the Mississippi Delta sharecropper's words. But the belief in a culture of poverty and cultural deprivation does not die easily. It remains an excellent excuse for class disparity and racism. By opening one's eyes to the hopes and aspirations of Black Americans, one could begin to recognize America's unequal distribution of wealth and its endemic racism.

Chapter 3

Visual Sociological Portrayals of Race and Childhood: Case Studies from the Thirties

I recently received an invitation to critique three narrative and visual presentations at the national meeting of the American Educational Research Association. One of the presentations described childhood and education in the thirties as depicted in James Agee and Walker Evans's classic book *Let Us Now Praise Famous Men*. The slides were moving and the narrative interesting, but the presentation was flawed. The problem was that the presenter wanted the audience to accept the Agee-Evans view of sharecropper children as the Depression reality. The presenter failed to acknowledge the many other narrative-visual portraits of Depression life. This discussion broadens the general impression of life in the thirties by introducing narrative-visual portrayals of African-American children in both rural and urban settings. My sources include Richard Wright's *12 Million Black Voices* (1941) and Stella Gentry Sharpe's *Tobe* (1939), as well as work that critically analyzes the narrative-visual documentation of the Depression (Sharpe, 1939; Wright, 1941; Stott, 1973; Watkins, 1982; and Puckett, 1984).

12 Million Black Voices

The photographic documentation of the Depression became the responsibility of the Historical Section of the Farm Security Administration. In his study, "The Blurred Image," Charles Watkins (1982) asserted that although FSA photographers took pictures of African-Americans, the government chose not to make the recording of Black life a priority:

> The result was that the Historical Section did a poor job of documenting discrimination against Blacks in the South, perhaps the major defining characteristic of the region. This was because Stryker's organization was not an autonomous unit, but only a small cog in the mighty New Deal machine. On the national level, the New Deal could not politically afford to allow powerful Southern Congressmen to believe that one of its agencies condoned the sending of camera-equipped snoopers into the South to pry into racial matters. . . . So, although the Historical Section was upset about the treatment of Blacks below the Mason-Dixon line, it had little opportunity to document or publicize it (pp. 317-318).

The head of the Historical Section, Roy Stryker, nonetheless sympathized with the need to document racial discrimination, and when the chance arose, he assigned Russell Lee to help Edwin Rosskam photograph African-American life in Chicago for *12 Million Black Voices*:

> The ostensible reason for sending Lee to a place where FSA clearly had no program interest was that Chicago was the terminal point for the migration of Black agricultural workers from the South and, therefore, urban photographs were needed to document the full story of Southern farm labor (p. 320).

This was a smokescreen; Stryker knew Richard Wright's work and was sympathetic to his cause. Wright experimented with Communism, and although he later condemned it, the tone of *12 Million Black Voices* is what I have called "soft socialism" (Wieder, 1979, pp. 255-262). His purpose was to show the innate goodness of Black Americans and the evils of an American system contaminated by racism. Wright fully intended to portray racism so as to inspire outrage in his readers.

Wright divided *12 Million Black Voices* (1941) into four sections. The first three describe slavery, southern rural life, and urban life in the North. The final section discusses hopes for a nation free of racism. The book includes 147 photographs, most taken by Russell Lee in Chicago. These photographs, selected by Rosskam, vividly illustrate Wright's message.

Wright began with the sea passage from freedom in Africa to slavery in America, and described the harshness of racism in the United States in the past and present. He analyzed the psychological and sociological burdens racism places on African-Americans and urged whites to realize that racism is a disease infecting all Americans:

> We Black folk, our history and our present being, are a mirror of all the manifold experiences of America. What we want, what we represent, what we endure is what America is. If we black folk perish, America will perish (p. 146).

Wright portrayed a world of racial war even in the best of times. Whites are divided into three groups: "Lords of the Land," "Bosses of Buildings," and poor whites. The first two rule and make sure Blacks and poor whites always remain at odds. It is a socialist perspective, and although Wright overemphasized his "Lords" and "Bosses" phrasing, his analysis is instructive. His descriptions of the hardship of African-American life are especially powerful because they explain how racism prevails even as whites claim moral superiority:

> This dual attitude, compounded of a love of gold and God, was the beginning of America's paternalistic code toward her Black maid, her Black industrial worker, her Black stevedore, her Black dancer, her Black waiter, her Black sharecropper; it was a code of casual cruelty, of brutal kindness, of genial despotism, a code which has survived,

Photo 1   Dorthea Lange: "Plantation Owner Mississippi."

Photo 2   Jack Delano: "Sharecroppers, Georgia."

grown, spread, and congealed into a national tradition that domi-
nates, in a small or large measure, all black and white relations throughout the nation until this day (pp. 17–18).

The focus of *12 Million Black Voices*, though, is the economic,
social and psychological burdens Blacks must endure in the
United States because of white racism. Dorthea Lange's photograph, "Plantation Owner," is a clear portrait of class and
race and power (photo 1). Jack Delano's photograph of sharecroppers portrays the harshness and the pain that white racism fosters (photo 2).

Wright's portrayal of childhood in *12 Million Black Voices* is
preceded by a description and critique of life in kitchenette
apartments in the urban Black ghettos. The African-American
migration from the South to the North in search of a better

life was personal for Wright. As a young man he journeyed to Chicago looking for the opportunities unavailable in the South, and all too often he found discrimination and squalor. The tenement apartments he described and Lee photographed portray the urban reality many African-Americans found as they migrated to Northern cities (photos 3, 4, and 5). Wright described the blockbusting and the "Bosses of Buildings" buying up apartments, and redividing them and inflating the rents for Black migrants without real choices to make. Sadly, Wright's description was repeated only recently by Jonathan Kozol, whose book *Rachel and Her Children* (1987) critiques life in America's welfare hotels. Wright and Kozol both describe landlords who charge exorbitant prices for unsafe and poorly maintained housing. As both authors make clear, children generally suffer the most.

Wright's first mention of children appeared in a discussion of the large African-American families in the rural South. He spoke of the need for more children to work in the fields, and he reiterated this idea when he discussed schooling:

Photo 3   Russell Lee: "Empty Lot and Houses, Chicago."

Photo 4   Russell Lee: "Interior of Kitchenette, Chicago."

> Sometimes there is a weather-worn, pine-built schoolhouse for our
> children, but even if the school were open for the full term our chil-
> dren would not have the time to go. We cannot let them leave the
> fields when cotton is waiting to be picked (p. 64).

Wright laid a heavy emphasis on large loving families, the
joys of having children, and the unbending loyalty of family
members toward each other. He recalled happy times of laugh-
ter and family singing and he emphasized the importance of
kinship. But he still stressed the difficulty of southern rural
life.

Wright's *12 Million Black Voices* is also critical of rural
schools. He, like Kozol much later, underlined the harsh inequality. Kozol's book, called *Savage Inequalities* (1991), de-

Photo 5   Russell Lee: "Negro Family, Chicago."

scribes the enormous disparity between suburban and urban public schools. Wright traced tax money paid by Black Americans flowing to schools only white children attend; he found the state of Mississippi spending five times as much on a white child as a Black child. He emphasized the great desire African-Americans have for their children to be educated, but he also made it clear that they are well aware of the injustices that pervade segregated education:

> Deep down we distrust the schools that the Lords of the Land build for us and we do not really feel that they are ours. In many states they edit the textbooks that our children study, for the most part deleting all references to government, voting, citizenship, and civil rights. Many of them say that French, Latin, and Spanish are languages not for us, and they become angry when they think that we desire to learn more than they want us to. They say that "all the geography a nigger needs to know is how to get from his shack to the plow." They restrict our education easily, inasmuch as their laws decree that there must be schools for our Black children and schools for the white, churches for our Black folk and churches for the white, and in public places their signs read: FOR COLORED and FOR WHITE (p. 64).

The injustices Wright described were even harsher in the city. He cries for the children who spend their days unattended because their mothers must work and for teenagers who drop out of school and find unemployment, desperation, and hopelessness in urban life. One long paragraph and a stark photograph by Edwin Rosskam (Photo 6) tell this story:

> We watch strange moods fill our children, and our hearts swell with pain. The streets, with their noise and flaring lights, the taverns, the automobiles, and the poolrooms claim them, and no voice of ours can call them back. They spend their nights away from home; they forget our ways of life, our language, our God. Their swift speech and impatient eyes make us feel weak and foolish. We cannot keep them in school; more than 1,000,000 of our black boys and girls of high school age are not in school. We fall upon our knees and pray for them, but in vain. The city has beaten us; but they with young bodies filled with warm blood, feel bitter and frustrated at the sight of the alluring hopes and prizes denied them. As the courts and the morgues become crowded with our lost children, the hearts of the officials of the city grow cold toward us. As our jobs begin to fail in another depression, our lives and the lives of our children grow so frightful that even some of our educated Black leaders are afraid to make known to the nation how we exist. And many white people who know how we live are afraid of us, fearing that we may rise up against them (p. 136).

Photo 6   Edwin Rosskam: "Boy in Front of Apartment House, Chicago."

Wright called the last section of *12 Million Black Voices* "Men in the Making." After discussing the racism that exists to this day, Wright spoke of African-Americans making it and of their hopes and aspirations: "We want what others have, the right to share in the upward march of American life, the only life we remember or have ever known" (p. 146).

Tobe

Stella Gentry Sharpe's book *Tobe* stands in stark contrast to the portrait of African-American life presented in *12 Million Black Voices*. In the late 1920s and 1930s, sociologist Howard Odum led the Institute for Research in Social Science at the University of North Carolina. The institute specialized in social, political, and economic issues in the South. *Tobe* was not part of the institute's work, nevertheless it became a major project for William Couch, the director of the University of North Carolina Press, who was influenced by Odum's work. Originally intended as a children's book, *Tobe* appealed to a far broader audience. In *The Blurred Image* (1982), his study of photographic portraits of the Depression, Charles Watkins reported that the book was well received by scholars, activists, and educators both in North Carolina and throughout the country. He listed these three major goals Sharpe had set out to achieve:

(1) to present Black children as "normal,"
(2) to enhance race relations by getting white children to understand Black children, and
(3) to put a good light on rural life (p. 322).

Stella Gentry Sharpe originally turned in her manuscript with Kodak snapshots she had taken of a sharecropper family. The snapshots showed the hard life and burdens of sharecropping, but Couch commissioned Charles Farrell to photograph the positive aspects of life for rural African-American children. Both the content and the style differ substantially from *12 Million Black Voices*. *Tobe* runs for 121 pages and, except for its first page where one finds text under a photograph of Tobe and his brothers, the layout places the text on the left and

Photo 7   By Charles Farrell from Tobe

Farrell's photographs on the right. Tobe introduces us to his family and his pets; he takes us to his school and his church; and we see him and his brothers at work and at play (photos 7 and 8). All of the photographs are wholesome, with none of the hardness or harshness of life set forth in Wright's book.

The description of the school is especially interesting when contrasted to Richard Wright's section on education. In *Tobe*, school and church are both extensions of the home:

> This is our school. We keep it nice and clean. We have trees in the yard. We are planting some bushes. When they grow, the yard will be pretty (p. 16).

Each of the short writings, whether they describe the school (photo 9) or the farm animals the children love, or a pet dog (photo 10), has the same tone: Life is wholesome, and it is wonderful to be alive.

It is even this way when Tobe discusses chores and work. Whether it is planting crops, harvesting wheat, gathering fruit, picking tobacco leaves, grubbing up sweet potatoes, picking cotton, or helping dad, the descriptions are always positive, upbeat. The closest Tobe comes to a complaint is when he mentions that cotton hurts when he picks it. Of course, when his mom explains that they get their clothing by selling cotton, Tobe's spirits rise: "I did not know that. . . . I will pick cotton"

Photo 8   By Charles Farrell from Tobe

(p. 58). The only hint of danger or discontent in the entire book comes when Tobe's mother teaches him how to ward off a bully by using a tin of pepper (photo 11). But even that episode suggests a wholesome, simple, rural life.

Finally, we find a description of Christmas with Santa Claus bringing gifts for the children. Santa's visit challenges the perception of unrelenting poverty and deprivation and dramatizes the rural Black positive life, which is the essence of *Tobe*. Unlike *12 Million Black Voices*, one finds no discussion of meaning, only both the visual and narrative portrayals of whole-

Photo 9   By Charles Farrell from Tobe

some African-American life, as told from the perspective of a young Black child.

Conclusion

12 Million Black Voices and *Tobe* are far from the only Depression portrayals of race available. Other texts on race in the Depression and additional photographs of African-Americans include for example, Stryker and Woods (1973), and Tyack,

Photo 10   By Charles Farrell from Tobe

Photo 11   By Charles Farrell from Tobe

Lowe and Hansot (1984). Some of these photographs, many from the Farm Security Administration collection, depict a middle ground, neither the harshness of Rosskam's selections nor the Pollyannish nature of Farrell's pictures. In fact, William Stott critiqued the harshness of Wright's book in *Documentary Expression and Thirties America* (1973):

> Wright's history, in deliberately ignoring the reality of the past, promulgates such dubious analogies as that between "the slavetraders" and "our contemporary 'captains of industry' and 'tycoons of finance.'" His whole effort is to shock, touch, enrage his audience, as he was enraged, and he used any means to this end (p. 235).

Charles Watkins also criticized *12 Million Black Voices*. He noted that even though Rosskam was alienated by the "holier-than-thou" attitude of Wright's text he chose to omit many of the photographs Russell Lee took of middle-class African-Americans in Chicago (p. 322). But Watkins criticized *Tobe* for its one-sided portrayal:

> *Tobe* also pretended that 300 years of white oppression of Blacks had never existed. By focusing on the happiness of Tobe's existence and the apparent well-being of his family, the book implied that there was equal opportunity for both races, certainly a distortion of fact (p. 337).

The principal question, though, remains: What makes the middle-ground portraits any more real than those at the extremes? Neither *12 Million Black Voices* nor *Tobe* presented the definitive statement on African-American life during the Depression. Instead, each book provided a portrait of a part of African-American life. Richard Wright's book is important because it accurately portrayed our country's historical and current racism. The photographs are powerful because they illustrate the ills that racism inflicts. *Tobe* is important because it depicts an African-American family attempting to live the American dream, a reality that has been and still is widely ignored. The photographs that illustrate *Tobe* compellingly portray the wholesomeness and decency of the boy's life.

Interestingly enough, Richard Wright concluded *12 Million Black Voices* with a plea for the life *Tobe* represents: "We want what others have, the right to share in the upward march of American life, the only life we remember or have ever known" (Wright, p. 146). The need remains for additional portraits. For now, let us consider two very different views that have yet to receive the attention they deserve. We each have our own biases. For the moment, however, it is unimportant whether we think Wright's work is more accurate than Sharpe's. What is important is that we examine a variety of portraits of Depression life and race so that we can broaden our view and that we examine portraits that may seem extreme for the truths they offer.

Chapter 4

Possibilities, Lost Possibilities, No Possibilities: Images of Middle-Class Children and Lower-Class Adults

Although the standard literature in social stratification and in the sociology of education documents racial disharmony and growing racial disparity, Americans continue to recite a belief in the American dream and the public school as the agent of economic equality. Public figures with ideologies as disparate as those of Pat Robertson and Jesse Jackson urge children to stay in school and reap the economic rewards schooling can provide. In some ways, their urgings echo the early-morning television commercials of the early 1960s informing the young how much money they would make in a lifetime if they stayed in school, compared to how little they would make if they dropped out.

The urge appears in such recent educational reform reports as *A Nation at Risk*. It is difficult to find public voices, on the left or the right, that argue with the vision of the American dream found in that report or the state-by-state educational reform acts that took shape in its wake. In South Carolina, for example, both Democrats and Republicans publicly proclaim that the Educational Improvement Act will help alleviate poverty in the state. But both federal and state education officials ignore the research that questions the ability of schools to alleviate poverty. Classics like *Who Gets Ahead* (Jencks et al., 1979) and the recent surge of such new books as *Plural But Equal*

(Cruse, 1987), *Racial Attitudes in America* (Schuman, Steeh, and Bobo, 1987), and *The Truly Disadvantaged* (Wilson, 1986) warn of growing class disparity and the impotence of schooling as an agent of equality. The following passage from Richard de Lone's Carnegie Foundation study, *Small Futures* (1978) may help humanize the issue:

> Jimmy is a second grader. He pays attention in school, and he enjoys it. School records show that he is reading slightly above grade level and has a slightly better than average IQ. Bobby is a second grader in a school across town. He also pays attention in class and enjoys school, and his test scores are quite similar to Jimmy's. Bobby is a safe bet to enter college (more than four times as likely as Jimmy) and a good bet to complete it — at least 12 times as likely as Jimmy. Bobby will probably have at least four years more schooling than Jimmy. He is 27 times as likely as Jimmy to land a job which by his late forties will pay him an income in the top tenth of all incomes. Jimmy has about one chance in eight of earning a median income.
>
> These odds are the arithmetic of inequality in America. They can be calculated with the help of a few more facts about Bobby and Jimmy. Bobby is a son of a successful lawyer whose annual salary puts him well within the top 10% of the United States income distribution. Jimmy's father, who did not complete high school, works from time to time as a messenger or a custodial assistant. His earnings put him in the bottom 10%. Bobby lives with his mother and father and sister. Jimmy lives with his father, mother, three brothers, and two sisters (pp. 3–4).

The images in the following photographic essay portray the disparity deLone (1978) studied in the United States. Poverty in the United States has been depicted photographically since the turn of the century. For example, Lewis Hine (1909) and Jacob Riis (1890) both documented tenement living and public schooling. The photographs of Walker Evans, Dorthea Lange, and Russell Lee (Stryker, 1973) provide visual portraits of the Depression. Only recently has this type of work begun to resurface in a field aptly named "visual sociology." This essay conforms to the tradition probably best represented today by Howard Becker's traveling show and subsequent book, *Exploring Society Photographically* (1981).

The images here contrast middle-class children and impoverished adults. The portraits are arranged to magnify the social and economic disparity in American society—the difference, that is, between hope and reality.

Figure 1a.
One-legged Man.
Columbia South Carolina,
1988.

Figure 1b.
Child of MTV.
Oshkosh, Wisconsin. 1985.

Figure 2a.
Man on Pickens Street.
Columbia, South Carolina,
1987.

Figure 2b.
Kids in Yard.
Oshkosh, Wisconsin, 1986.

Figure 3a
Woman in Window.
New York City, 1976.

Figure 3b.
Ariel.
Newark, Delaware, 1987.

Figure 4a.
Man at Parade.
Columbia, South Carolina,
1987.

Figure 4b.
Nathan.
Asheville, North Carolina,
1987.

Figure 5a.
Resting-Alan's Photography.
Atlanta, Georgia, 1985.

Figure 5b.
Joel in Pot.
Oshkosh, Wisconsin, 1985

Chapter 5

Common Ground:
A Review of Reviews

This chapter presents a review of the reviews of *Common Ground* (1985), J. Anthony Lukas's extensive oral history of school integration in Boston. *Common Ground* has won the National Book Award and the Pulitzer Prize and has since been reviewed extensively in popular journals. It also became the basis for a miniseries subsequently shown on network television. *Common Ground* remains our most important oral history of school integration, and it also exemplifies the possibilities of connecting educational history and oral history. It has been twenty-four years since William Cutler's *History of Education Quarterly* article invited educational historians to use oral history, and few of us have answered the invitation. Neil Sutherland's work on childhood in Vancouver, Maxine Seller's studies in Buffalo, Richard Altenbaugh's work on teachers in Pittsburgh, Richard Quantz's work in Ohio, Mary Jo Deering's Baltimore studies, and Kim Rogers' and my own desegregation projects in New Orleans are the only projects that come to mind. Luckily, Lukas's popularity and craftsmanship will surely provide educational historians with an appropriate and timely model.

The Book

Lukas spent seven years researching school desegregation in Boston. The media covered the Boston school crisis extensively and television brought the violence in South Boston and Charlestown into our homes each night. Boston is remembered, with Little Rock and New Orleans, for the white racism and violence that accompanied desegregation. *Common Ground*, though, takes a reader far beyond the media-portrayed violence. Lukas tells the story of school desegregation through the lives of three families who were both involved in and deeply affected by the event. The relationship of the three families— the Divers (WASP liberals), the Twymons (Blacks), the McGoffs, (Irish people opposed to busing)—and the desegregation efforts in the city form the core of the book. One also finds portraits of Judge W. Arthur Garrity who ruled in favor of school busing, Mayor Kevin White, *Boston Globe* editor Thomas Winship, school committee member and anti-busing advocate Louise Day Hicks, and Cardinals Cushing and Mederos.

Readers get to know these public people mainly through their relationships to the school crisis. They get to know far more about the Divers, Twymons, and McGoffs as Lukas explores the personal side of school desegregation in Boston. He builds to the stories of the three families and desegregation by tracing them through three generations. Lukas represents what I have previously called "the oral historian as artist." His portrayals of the three families and others are finely crafted and answer a need generally present in educational history—a need for the interactive and personal approach.

The Reviews

After rereading *Common Ground*, I examined eleven reviews of the book. All eleven credit Lukas as a master storyteller, but some see his storytelling as a limitation. Lukas, himself, has acknowledged some of the gentle reproaches. He offered this observation in a National Public Radio interview: "Some people have said, 'Ah, come on Lukas, we know what the Divers, McGoffs, and Twymons think. What about you, chap? Take a stand."

The reviewers who were most critical of Lukas wanted more than just a stand. They have noted Lukas's penchant for storytelling and his omission of facts and ideas and issues, and they used their reviews to write his final chapter. Mark Zanger, writing in *The Nation* (October 5, 1985), makes his purpose very clear:

> Those of us who review *Common Ground* end up finding it incomplete. We use our review space to describe the lessons of Boston, in effect writing our own introductions to the book. Here's mine (p. 317).

Not surprisingly, "our own introductions" equates to "our own ideology." Zanger's review and George Robinson's review in *The Progressive* (March, 1986) represent the left. The right receives its say in *National Review* and *Commentary* reviews, the former by Thomas McDonnell and the latter by James Q. Wilson.

Robinson's *Progressive* review is actually quite gentle. The "soft socialist" social engineering mentality of *The Progressive* is, however, obvious:

> Therein lies one of the anguishing things about the book. As Lukas writes, the problems of neighborhoods were systematic, rooted in intractable dilemmas of race and class, while downtown could be treated with quick infusions of cash and chic. [The] easy way out is the one taken by Kevin White, Ed Koch, and most other big-city mayors. Sadly, Lukas offers no hope of another, more human solution. Granted it is not the work of a journalist, however skilled, to take on the mantle of the urban planner, but when reading a book as depressingly detailed as *Common Ground*, one yearns for a little solace (p. 44).

Like Robinson, Zanger goes easy on Lukas. He praises the presentation of the many viewpoints, but at the same time, he yearns for analysis deriving from and extending beyond Lukas's narrative. Although he gives "Lukas's lives" credence for stating themes—the connection of social class and race for example—he fears that the book's lack of analysis leads to a leveling of issues:

> It still wants interpretation to avoid two common misreadings. The first can be seen in the tendency of reviewers to summarize the Boston situation as a failure of mutual understanding. . . . The other and opposite misreading entails the superstition that Boston had inevitably to be racist and violent (p. 317).

If we push Zanger's "misreading number one," racism gets lost in a multitude of personalities and issues. Michael Frisch made the same case in his reviews of recent Viet Nam War oral histories. Although the use of personalities in objective histories is an important consideration, it is not at issue in *Common*

Ground. Because we get to know and might even have compassion for the McGoffs does not mean that we excuse their racism.

The second problem, according to Zanger, is that Lukas's lengthy history makes racism in Boston appear inevitable, and he disagrees:

> I can tell you that real people with free will lived in Boston the whole time. The historical undertow was rough, but we sank or swam on our own. We were dumb; we were without leadership; we were hog swaggled by race and class and dogma (p. 317).

For Zanger, the strident anti-busing people—the Louise Day Hickses of the world—are not the issue. The real issue, which he feels gets lost in *Common Ground*, is the failure of the liberal leadership—Kevin White and his men. It is the perfect critique for *The Nation*: The liberals wanted the best of all worlds, they wanted Black support, white ethnic support, and white liberal support and they ended up making incremental moves that exacerbated the racial and class disparity instead of facilitating peaceful school integration. Where Mrs. Hicks might play the part of Sartre's conservative bigot, Mayor White could certainly audition for the liberal bigot role. Zanger should have pushed this point, but Lukas's portrait of the mayor actually did it quite well. Has the left, or at least Zanger's representation of the left, failed to understand storytelling?

Thomas McDonnell's essay in *National Review* (December 13, 1985) got the award for strident ideology. He tells us that the problem is the book hides the central secrets of school busing:

(1) Boston schools have reached a reverse imbalance;
(2) The evil government has, again, put the screws to poor Blacks while Irish-suburbanites remain unscathed; and
(3) Liberals are the real problem and besides that, they have demonstrated a functional stupidity.

McDonnell's first two secrets are hardly hidden. Although the current racial imbalance in urban education is certainly an important issue, it has little to do with *Common Ground*. Lukas addressed McDonnell's second secret more than once in his book. Compare the following two excerpts, the first from McDonnell:

> The truth of the matter is that the social experiment indulged by the courts was not suffered by the WASP community, nor by the Jewish community, nor even by the predominantly Italian North End; It was suffered by the two communities that were least able to deal with it on both economic and historical grounds (p. 42).

The second is from Lukas:

> Students increasingly came from the lowest economic and social strata of the city's population. More and more, Boston's busing program consisted of mixing the Black poor with the white poor, the deprived with the deprived (p. 650).

Although Lukas chose not to stress the evils of government intervention, he raises the issue of poor Blacks and poor whites shouldering the burdens of integration. McDonnell not withstanding, much of his portrayal of the Twymons and McGoffs explores this very issue.

McDonnell's liberal flaying becomes excessive. Although one can certainly question liberal involvement in social issues, McDonnell simply ignored Lukas's portrayal of the Divers. While Lukas's depth makes it impossible to reduce his characters to cultural stereotypes, McDonnell does not have the same problem. For him:

> Colin and Joan Diver are not only the most pathetic element to be found in *Common Ground*, but prove to be fairly irrelevant as well; They are muddle-headed suburban progressives who get in the way of solving any problem at hand (p. 42).

A review in *The New Leader* by Barry Gewen (November 4, 1985) provides an interesting contrast:

> The Divers made an admirable choice compared to the legions of doctors, lawyers, and MBA's who get their degrees already wondering how they are going to invest their first million. . . . About the Divers, at least we can say they tried (p. 14).

The second conservative review, James Q. Wilson's piece in *Commentary* (January, 1986), eschews rhetoric and commonplaces. Wilson criticizes Lukas for his failure to take a stand:

> But Lukas' resolute refusal to judge—save here and there by slips of
> the pen—makes us wonder who can ever hope to judge, since it is
> unlikely anyone will ever again interview as many people and read as
> many documents as did Lukas (p. 68).

Like Zanger, Wilson wanted Lukas to write a different book.
The current fate of Boston's schools is one of the themes Wilson wanted Lukas to develop. The major focus of Wilson's review, though, is Judge Garrity. While Zanger takes Lukas to
task for his treatment of Mayor White, Wilson takes him to
task for being lenient with the judge. Wilson is clear about
how he thinks the judge should be portrayed: "Judge Garrity
very nearly destroyed the Boston public schools as a conse-
quence of an insensitive, heavy handed, overly intrusive desegregation plan" (p. 68).

Wilson continues by listing Judge Garrity's faults, his major
sin being an insistence on massive busing. Wilson clarifies
neither the course of the near destruction of the Boston schools
nor what conditions existed prior to the busing initiative. He
criticized Lukas simply for neglecting to condemn the judge;
he himself neglects to mention that Lukas seems supportive of
Garrity's action. One must conclude that the reviewer, like
many of the other reviewers, missed much of the essence of
Lukas's narrative.

Two welcome exceptions are essays by Robert Coles and Jack
Beatty. In *Washington Monthly* (September, 1985), Coles addresses the marriage of methodology and substance in Lukas's
work; in *Atlantic Monthly* (September, 1985) Beatty outlines the
issues Lukas's portraits raise. Coles understands that the primary job of oral history is telling of the story:

> His "research methodology" was quite simple: go and find a few fami-
> lies, get to know them well, tell others their stories—what happened
> to certain people in their minds and hearts as they became in their
> own ways, historical actors, if not protagonists of sorts (p. 10).

Of course Coles' "simple methodology" can be difficult to ex-
ecute. Telling the stories of a few families means interacting
with those families; it means coming to know them as well as
the theme of discussion—in this case desegregation in Boston—
well enough to tell their stories. Coles gives Lukas credit:

He demonstrates a brilliant and subtle narrative skill—the ability to offer not just piecemeal accounts of black urban life up north, or of the fierce white resistance to court-ordered busing, or of the vicissitudes of upper middle class idealism, but a thoroughly coherent overall view of how individuals get caught (and hurt or challenged to new levels of personal and ethical achievement) by the political and cultural changes that take place in their lives (p. 10).

Jack Beatty's review analyzes the issues that Lukas's lives raise. Unlike the critiques of the left and right cited earlier, Beatty's issues are the same ones included in *Common Ground*.

Three major themes emerge: values, economics, and class. Beatty takes one detour. He raises a friend's question, "Why did Lukas have to pick a Black family that embodies everything whites fear about poor ghetto Blacks?" (p. 109). The Twymons' story is important, but might Lukas have also portrayed a Black family from the bourgeoisie? While we are on the topic, a liberal pro-busing Irish family might also have added a valuable perspective.

The first issue Beatty raises, values, is addressed throughout *Common Ground*. Two conflicting American beliefs, equality and community, are present in the portrayal of all three families as well as the supporting players. The second issue, economics, is similarly ubiquitous. The unemployment and hard times of Bostonians, white and Black, are very much a part of life for both the Twymons and the McGoffs. The economic reality leads to Beatty's third issue, social class. The people directly affected by desegregation in Boston (as well as in other cities) were working-class and lower-class people. Beatty points out that the busing failed to cross Boston class lines.

We do use poor Blacks and whites for our social experiments: In my own work in New Orleans soon to be discussed, I came across a speech Ralph McGill, then editor of the *Atlanta Constitution*, made to the New Orleans school board before desegregation in the city. He warned them not to integrate only the poor areas of the city. He explained that lower-class people already faced inadequate roads, garbage collection, and public services. They felt exploited, and desegregation might force them over the edge. In spite of the warning, New Orleans, like Boston, initially integrated only working-class and lower-class schools.

Conclusion

The issues Beatty discusses receive a thorough presentation in *Common Ground*. Together, Coles's methodological review and Beatty's issue-oriented review portray Lukas's book as the productive oral history he meant to write. Lukas tells us an important story with depth and insight. *Common Ground* is far more than a string of anecdotes. Lukas's interaction with the people he portrays (the interviewer–interviewee relationship) makes their stories come alive. His involvement with his people's lives establishes *Common Ground* as valuable oral history. With *Common Ground* as model, it is time to reissue Cutler's invitation to oral history. It can only broaden our scope as educational historians.

SECTION TWO

INTRODUCTORY NOTE

I wrote and published my oral histories of school integration in New Orleans throughout the eighties to show both the racial hatred and human struggle that accompanied school integration following the *Brown* decision. Throughout these histories I introduce people who sacrificed a great deal in the fight for racial equality. At the time these histories began to first appear, school integration had been the law of the land for thirty years, yet in many places, including New Orleans, schools remained racially segregated. In spite of the *Brown* decision and the many well-publicized battles for school integration, and in spite of the fact that Black people and white people alike sacrificed a great deal for school integration, many American children continue to attend racially segregated schools even as we approach the twenty-first century.

Chapter 6

The New Orleans School Crisis of 1960:
Causes and Consequences

On November 14, 1960, New Orleans began its initial token effort at school desegregation. Two elementary schools, McDonough 19 and Frantz, became the first New Orleans schools since Reconstruction to integrate their classrooms. New Orleanians viewed themselves and the city as cosmopolitan and tolerant and they assumed that the sophisticated nature of the city made it a model Southern city for school integration. The city had integrated public transit and the public library without incident, and as I reported in 1984, New Orleanians were proud of race relations in the city:

> The races had always lived very amicably. Blacks and whites had always lived in mixed neighborhoods. New Orleans is pretty much that way and it has always been a live and let live atmosphere (p. 195).

Much to their embarrassment, however, school desegregation was anything but amicable. Whites from the two integrated schools removed their children en masse, and racial violence sprang up throughout the city.

Two major reasons have been offered for what locals reluctantly refer to as "the New Orleans school crisis of 1960." The first is outside agitation; the second is the failure of the city's elite to promote integration. This chapter reviews each position briefly and then broadens the perspective by offering a narrative history of the ten years that preceded the crisis.

Outside Agitation

Blaming outside agitators for the school boycott and the racial violence fomented by whites conforms to the arguments opponents of integration make. The principal of one of the two integrated schools nevertheless told me it was a major influence (1986):

> They said that the pressures out there were too great. They didn't know what to do. There was tremendous community pressure and being as close as that school is to St. Bernard and Perez. There was a lot of pressure from the WCC people of this world (p. 125).

For Principal Stewart, "outside influence" meant the White Citizens Council and Plaquemine Parish boss Leander Perez. Both Glenn Jeansomme's book, *Leander Perez: Boss of the Delta*, and Morton Inger's *Politics and Reality* refer to Perez's speech at the November 15 meeting of the White Citizens Council: "Don't wait for your daughter to be raped by these Congolese. Don't wait until the burrheads are forced into your schools. Do something about it now" (*Times Picayune*, November 16, 1960, p. 2).

Violence followed the next day, Perez's speech among others having been received as a call to action. Perez also used his wealth and influence to offer the whites at McDonough 19 and Frantz an alternative to integration, an offer fully documented in the report of the Louisiana Advisory Committee to the United States Civil Rights Commission. When United States marshals escorted three Black children into McDonough 19 and one Black child into Frantz, white parents whose children attended the schools acted quickly. By 11:30 a.m. only a handful of white children remained in attendance. The white parents experienced a great deal of confusion, but Perez helped ease the problem. He donated a building and the money to open a private school, the Ninth Ward Cooperative School, for kindergarten through third grade, and he used his influence to get the St. Bernard schools, in the parish adjoining McDonough 19 and Frantz, to enroll their fourth through sixth graders.

Thus Jack Stewart and others contend that without Perez's involvement there would have been little violence and no successful boycott. Certainly the White Citizens Council meeting aroused many people, and one doubts street rioting would have occurred had the meeting not taken place. Certainly the Ninth Ward Cooperative School and the opening of the St. Bernard schools gave white parents an educational option. We do not know whether the parents would have returned their children to the integrated schools had Perez not acted.

The Failure of the Elite

The general failure of the elite to support school integration is the theme of Inger's book *Politics and Reality*. The idea is reiterated by one of the city's elite, Betty Wisdom. Inger analyzed the elite in Southern cities and labels the New Orleans elite "traditional" as opposed to the "progressive" elite of Houston and Atlanta. He cited the silence of the local newspaper, *The Times Picayune*, to document the inaction of the elite. *The Atlanta Constitution*, on the other hand, became a vocal supporter of school integration in that city. He also noted that the elite of Dallas, Atlanta, Newark, and Montgomery acted as desegregation boosters in contrast to the New Orleans elite, who remained silent. Betty Wisdom explained this to me in 1983:

> Then there was the business community, the community leaders. The activists, particularly Save Our Schools, were their wives, daughters, and sisters. They could have done something to help. The paper would have listened to them, the mayor and the police would have listened to them. They were told repeatedly what would happen if no leadership was exerted by them. But they said nothing.

Easily as much as outside agitation, the failure of the New Orleans elite to act became an important element in the school crisis. Again, though, the story is still more extensive and complicated than a product of outside agitation, or a result of the failure of the elite, or both.

The Origins of School Desegregation in New Orleans: 1951–1960

On November 6, 1951, Black community leaders Leontine Luke and Wilbert Aubert called a meeting of the Ninth Ward Civic and Improvement League. In the late 1940s the League had begun lobbying the Orleans Parish School Board for equal school facilities for Blacks. They had wanted the board to honor *Plessy* v *Ferguson* and its "separate but equal" doctrine. But to no one's surprise, the Board remained unresponsive. Kim Rogers (1982) phrased it this way:

> The Negro public schools were dramatically inferior to white institutions. Negro petitioners repeatedly objected to the aged and overcrowded buildings, excessive student teacher ratios, and inadequate curricular offerings common in black public schools. The board ignored their requests and used its resources to construct and improve white schools (p. 45).

The November Civic and Improvement League meeting was held at Macarty School, an all-Black school evincing the "aged and overcrowded" conditions just described. Mrs. Luke and Mr. Aubert sought to solicit parent volunteers for a class action desegregation suit against the Orleans Parish School Board. Ninety-five parents volunteered; and on September 5, 1952, A. P. Tureaud, chief legal council for the local chapter of the National Association for the Advancement of Colored People (NAACP), filed *Bush* v *Orleans Parish School Board*. The suit had two purposes: first to make a case for the unconstitutionality of segregation; and second, if the court found segregation legal, to ask the Orleans Parish School Board to conform to the "separate but equal" precedent.

Although *Bush* was filed in 1952, it was the 1954 *Brown* case that finally overturned *Plessy* v *Ferguson* and made school desegregation the law of the land. The national office of the NAACP asked Tureaud to postpone the *Bush* case. Its staff had decided to try *Bush* after a final decision on *Brown* v *Topeka*. The NAACP had earlier built strong cases for the unconstitutionality of segregated schools in the South Carolina case of *Briggs* v *Elliot*, in the Virginia case of *Davis* v *County School Board of Prince Edward County*, in the Delaware case of *Gebhart* v *Belton*, and in the Kansas case of *Brown* v *Board of Education of Topeka*. The Supreme Court had consolidated them all as *Brown* v *Topeka*. The Court ruled segregated schools unconstitutional 1954. In 1955, the Court ruled in *Brown II* that schools were to be integrated "with all deliberate speed."

New Orleans and Louisiana were no different than the rest of the country regarding "with all deliberate speed." White supremacists like Plaquemines Parish District Attorney Leander Perez, State Senator William Rainach and Orleans Parish School board member Emile Wagner, however, interpreted "all deliberate speed" as "never." Others in the New Orleans business community, political figures including Mayor DeLessups Morrison, and the four remaining members of the school board viewed "all deliberate speed" as not too soon. The NAACP interpreted it as "now." In the fall of 1955, as A. P. Tureaud was asking Judge Skelly Wright to rule on the *Bush* case, the White Citizens Council was presenting a petition signed by fifteen thousand people to the Orleans Parish School Board. As M. L. Muller (1975) observed:

> In typical Citizen's Council rhetoric, the petition attacked the evils of integration, citing medical statistics which claimed to show that of those patients treated for venereal disease an over-whelming number were "colored." Thus, the petition urged that every possible action be taken to prevent the mixing of white and 'colored' children (p. 44).

On February 15, 1956, Judge Wright ruled Louisiana's segregation laws invalid, and he ordered the Orleans Parish School Board to submit a school integration plan. Judge Wright's ruling on the state's segregation laws referred to 1955 and 1956 laws passed in reaction to the *Brown* decision. As soon as the *Brown* decision came down, State Senator William Rainach initiated a legislative committee for the continuance of school segregation. In Rainach's words, desegregation would "plunge the white school children of Louisiana into moral and intellectual chaos and would seriously jeopardize their health" (*Times Picayune*, August 31, 1960, p. 1). Bills introduced by Rainach's committee and passed by the Louisiana legislature included a statute that made school integration grounds for firing principals and teachers. The legislature also banned interracial athletic and social events. Finally, it passed a bill that gave itself the power to define certain schools as Negro and others as white. Judge Wright would have occasion to invalidate these and subsequent Louisiana statutes throughout the late 1950s and early 1960s.

The Orleans Parish School Board decided to fight Judge Wright's decision. Board member Emile Wagner, Senator Rainach's close friend, was as strident a believer in segregation as either Rainach or Perez. Although the other board members were not White Citizens Council members and avoided public posturing, none of them supported integration. When the board's attorney, Samuel Rosenberg, advised it against fighting Judge Wright's decision, it chose another attorney. The board decided to join the state and fight integration and appointed Gerald Rault, a banking colleague of Emile Wagner, as its special legal counsel to fight Judge Wright. Rault received assistance from Leander Perez, and the two of them appealed all the way up to the Supreme Court. But in May of 1958, the highest court in the land upheld Wright's rulings. Rault advised the school board to ignore the decision, the state continued to pass anti-integration laws, and the NAACP insisted that Judge Wright implement integration. On July 15, 1959, he ordered the Orleans Parish School Board to present a desegregation plan by no later than March 1, 1960. In October 1959, he met with the school board's attorney, Gerald Rault, and the local NAACP attorney, A. P. Tureaud, and extended the deadline to May 16. When the school board failed to meet the deadline, Judge Wright issued this statement:

It is ordered that, beginning with the opening of school in September 1960, all public schools shall be desegregated in accordance with the following plan:
A. All children entering the first grade may attend either the former all-white public school nearest their homes or formerly all-negro public school nearest their homes, at their option.
B. Children may be transferred from one school to another provided such transfers are not based on consideration of race (Louisiana Advisory Committee, p. 5).

The Orleans Parish School Board, the Superintendent of Schools Dr. James Redmond, and the white parents of New Orleans viewed Judge Wright's plan as catastrophic. Could it be that Judge Wright wanted his plan viewed as such? Did he see his statement as the only way to get the Orleans Parish School Board to initiate action? Judge Wright knew, as did Superintendent Redmond, that many Negroes lived closer to white schools than to the Black schools they were attending.

Redmond and the board feared that Blacks would overrun previously all white schools. Muller analyzed the social geography this way:

> With approximately 7,000 Negro and 4,000 white first graders affected by the plan, white parents were acutely aware of the almost two-to-one situation their children faced if school officials freely and fairly carried out Judge Wright's order. School maps indicated just how thorough the mixing of these 11,000 children could be. Twenty-eight of the city's forty-eight white elementary schools had Negroes living closer to them than to the nearest Negro school, and nearly two-thirds of the city's white elementary schools had Negroes living close enough to warrant their admission under Judge Wright's plan (p. 56).

At the June 20 meeting of the Orleans Parish School Board, angry white parents protested Judge Wright's plan. But two organizations, Save Our Schools, a pro-integration group, and the Committee for Public Education, a parent's group for open schools, asked the board to submit a sensible desegregation plan. Six days later the Fifth District Court of Appeals rejected the school board's request to stay the desegregation order, and the board asked Governor Jimmy Davis, whose principal claim to fame remains as the country-western-gospel singer who wrote "You Are My Sunshine," to seize the schools. He was more than happy to oblige. The courts subsequently struck down his interposition and ordered him not to interfere with the New Orleans schools. Three days later, August 29, 1960, four of the five school board members—the lone dissenter remained Emile Wagner—met with Judge Wright to discuss submitting a plan. Their views were best expressed by the president of the board, Lloyd Rittiner:

> I am a segregationist—if, however, I am faced with a choice of integrating or closing, I am already on record as favoring integration to the extent that it is necessary to comply with the law—I think closing would be a mistake. If you have an integrated school system, the people would have a choice; but, if the schools were closed, there would be no choice. I don't think most people could afford the private schools, and I don't know what other solution there is (Louisiana Advisory Board, p. 4).

The board asked Judge Wright to delay desegregation until November 14 and he agreed. In turn, the board agreed to work out a desegregation plan. By beginning the school year as a segregated system, it hoped to ease the transition to "token" integration. Both white and Black students would be already settled in their respective schools and the board felt that most parents would want their children to remain there. Thus, few Blacks would want to integrate and those whites whose schools were integrated would be less liable to leave. The board told Superintendent Redmond to work out a plan in accordance with the state's pupil placement law, which gave school boards the sole authority to determine where a child could attend school. It assured only limited integration, in near contravention of Judge Wright's plan.

In spite of the limited integration the board's plan would allow, Wagner and special attorney Rault remained opposed. With the backing of the governor, the state legislature, and Leander Perez, Wagner continued to fight for the status quo. Gerald Rault resigned his position with the school board. The board began to outline what Morton Inger, with tongue in cheek, called "School Integration the Scientific Way."

The board claimed objectivity even as it appeared to lose all rationality, especially in regard to the schools it chose to be integrated first. Two uptown schools, Lusher and Wilson, had taken Parent Teacher Association votes and both had volunteered to lead the way. Meanwhile, as we have seen, Save Our Schools brought the editor of *The Atlanta Constitution*, Ralph McGill, to town to discuss integration. McGill, of course, warned the school board not to limit integration to a lower socioeconomic section of town. He predicted that poor people would feel patronized and to single them out would be to consign integration to the poor. But in the name of "scientific integration," the board turned down Lusher and Wilson and did exactly what McGill warned it not to do. The schools selected were both in the same lower and lower-middle-class neighborhood.

Students were allowed to apply for transfer in October and 136 applicants came forward. Robert Crain outlined the board's subsequent reassignment criteria in *The Politics of School Desegregation* (1969):

> Step One: Consideration by Four Assistant Superintendents of:
> *   Verification of information on application.
> *   Proper age (Birth Certificate).

* Nearness of school to child's home.
* Request or consent of parent and reasons assigned thereto.
* Available room and teaching capacity of schools.
* Availability of transportation.

Step Two: Consideration by the Acting Director of Guidance and Testing, psychologists, and psychometrists of:
* Scholastic aptitude.
* Intelligence or ability.
* Results of achievement.

Step Three: Consideration by the Assistant Superintendent for Instruction, the Director of Special Services, the Director of Kindergarten-Primary Education, psychologists, and visiting teachers of:
* Effect of new pupil upon the academic program.
* Suitability of established curricula for pupil.
* Adequacy of pupil's academic preparation or readiness for admission to school or curricula.
* Psychological qualification of pupil for type of teaching and associations.
* Effect upon academic progress of other students.
* Effect upon prevailing academic standards.
* Psychological effect upon the pupil.
* Home environment of the pupil.
* Maintenance or severance of social and psychological relationships with pupils and teachers.

Step Four: Consideration by an administrative review team composed of the Superintendent, the First Assistant Superintendent, the Acting Assistant Superintendent for Instruction and the school system's Medical Director of:
* All information previously collected on each applicant.
* Choice and interests of pupil.
* Possibility of threat of friction or disorder among pupils or others.
* Possibility of breach of peace or ill will or economic retaliation within the community (pp. 260–261).

Bear in mind that New Orleans adopted these criteria to judge first graders: six year olds. Moreover, one of the most fundamental criteria, sex, is missing from the list. When all of the applications were evaluated, five Black children were selected to integrate the Orleans Parish schools. All five were girls. Subsequent events in southern Louisiana proved this to be no coincidence. One adjoining parish, Jefferson, discontinued sexual segregation in its schools in the early eighties, and a second neighbor, St. Bernard Parish, continued to segregate its students by sex until the late eighties. Race and sex intermingle in the racist fears of white America, and as Crain noted, before New Orleans businessmen would lend even token support to the board's plan, they demanded sexual segregation:

> They would offer their assistance only if the board would separate the first grades by sex and keep the toilets in the schools segregated by race. Rittiner saw nothing wrong with separating the first-graders by sex—all the New Orleans schools had at one time been so divided—but he rejected the idea of segregating the toilets. The meeting ended at this point, and these men did not come out in favor of peace until several months after desegregation (p. 262).

Sex remained prominent in the thoughts of those New Orleans whites contemplating school desegregation. This local issue receives further attention in Kim Lacy Rogers's work and in the thorough discussion of white racism and sex in the United States presented in Joel Kovel's *White Racism: A Psychohistory* (1970).

In spite of overt sexual segregation and not-so-subtle legislative attempts to keep the Orleans Parish schools racially segregated, November 14 rapidly approached. At its November 10 meeting, school board president Lloyd Rittiner officially announced that in four days five Black children would enroll in two previously all-white schools. Supposedly the identities of the children and their schools were known only to the Orleans Parish School Board, but Mary Lee Muller (1975) has questioned this assumption:

> On November 8, two days before the school board announcement that five Negro girls would enter two "receiving" schools, Senator Robert Ainsworth of New Orleans, in a speech before the senate, said that the PTA of one of the two schools to have token integration voted to go along with token integration for the time being rather than close schools (p. 102).

Senator Ainsworth might have mistaken Lusher or Wilson for one of the two schools to be integrated, but my own interviews raised some questions regarding the overall secrecy. Armand Duvio, president of the Frantz School Fathers Club in 1960, told me that they "got word" that Frantz was to be integrated.

In any case the last weekend before New Orleans schools integrated was alive with preparation. Friday, November 11, was Veterans Day, an official school holiday. Superintendent Redmond summoned the principals of the two schools to be integrated, Jack Stewart of McDonough 19 and Estelle Barkemeyer of Frantz, to a meeting at which he informed them that their schools would be integrated Monday. On Saturday, November 12, the State Superintendent of Schools, Shelby Jackson, declared November 14 a state-wide school holiday. Betty Wisdom spoke with me about the absurdity of this declaration:

> Because the state constitution required 180 days of schooling and the closure would violate that, the legislature voted that for the purposes of law, the schools closed on The Day would be counted as open.

In fact, the Orleans Parish schools were the only schools in Louisiana to open on November 14, 1960.

Governor Davis and the state legislature also stood ready to make their last stand. At a special session called for Sunday, November 13, the legislature passed thirty bills, mostly reenactments of the bills Judge Wright had previously ruled unconstitutional. Included was an interposition bill to give the state sole power over its public schools, and bills giving the governor the right to close integrated schools, giving the legislature the right to cut off funding for all integrated schools, giving the governor the right to seize books at integrated schools, rescinding state accreditation of integrated schools, giving the legislature control of the Orleans Parish Schools, calling for the loss of teaching credentials for teachers teaching in integrated schools, giving the legislature the power to sell closed integrated schools, and revoking the 180-day minimum school year. But by Sunday evening, the Fifth District Court of Appeals had ruled all thirty statutes unconstitutional.

Additional events transpired on Sunday evening. The five Black children chosen to integrate schools received official notification of their selection. Both school principals received two telegrams. The first, from the federal government, informed them that their schools would be integrated the next morning. The second, from the state, informed them that if they opened integrated schools they would be arrested for contempt of the state legislature. Both chose to obey the federal government's telegram, and New Orleans began token school integration the next morning.

Discussion and Conclusions

School desegregation in New Orleans was neither peaceful nor successful. Black children and their families were harassed by crowds at both schools, and violence erupted throughout the city. The white boycott of McDonough 19 was complete; and by the end of the school year, only two white families remained at Frantz. Although integration proceeded throughout the sixties, schools in New Orleans remain segregated to this day, and the city continued to ignore its racial reality throughout the sixties and seventies. Just as the legal struggles of Blacks in the fifties were ignored, the school crisis was forgotten. Not until 1983 (and the election of a Black mayor) was the event acknowledged and the four Black women who integrated the New Orleans schools honored.

The irony is, of course, that their children attend segregated schools. One could easily conclude that New Orleans has failed so far to achieve school integration for the same reason that its school crisis occurred in the first place: the hesitancy of the white elite, and a white racism that crossed class lines. The struggle of Blacks for integrated schools, the resistance of whites at the two schools, the rioting of whites in the streets, the recalcitrance of the governor and state legislature, the initial obdurance of the school board—they all leave one with the impression that a great many white New Orleanians hated the thought of school integration. White racism was very much a part of New Orleans in the fifties, and the public schools were the last bastion of white superiority. The New Orleans school crisis makes sense when viewed in relationship to the racial struggles that preceded it, and those struggles still go on.

Chapter 7

One Who Stayed:
Margaret Conner and
the New Orleans School Crisis

On November 14, 1960, two New Orleans elementary schools—McDonogh 19 and Frantz in the Ninth Ward, a lower and lower-middle-class district—became racially integrated. The district included individually owned homes, some of which had housed the same families for three generations. It also held two public housing projects, Desire, which was white, and Florida, which was Black. Blacks and whites had lived near one another for a long time and generally got along well, but their schools had a long history of segregation. The segregation ended when three Black children were escorted by United States marshals into McDonogh 19 School. By the end of the school day, November 14, few white children remained at the school. Within a couple of days the population of McDonogh 19 consisted of the principal, the secretary, the custodian, eighteen teachers, and the three Black children.

A fourth Black child, Ruby Bridges, enrolled in Frantz School that same morning, effectively reducing the white enrollment there to between three and ten children. A few Baptist seminarians tried to keep their children in the school, but they eventually succumbed to the crowd harassment and nuisance phone calls. Their part-time jobs at Schwegmann Brothers, a popular local grocery chain, were also threatened. Two other parents who kept their children in school received a great deal of local and national media attention. The Reverend Andrew Foreman, a Methodist minister, was interviewed at various times and was televised daily as he escorted his five-year-old daughter Pam through the crowds. Mrs. Daisy Gabrielle received the same sort of attention. Her nobility caught the fancy of the media. But the physical, psychological, and economic pressures forced the family to return to Mr. Gabrielle's hometown in Rhode Island where employment was guaranteed. In the end, only two white families continued to send their children to Frantz School. The Conners were one of those families.

I visited with Margaret Conner in her suburban New Orleans apartment in the fall of 1982. She lives there alone. Her apartment is part of a multi-building complex, and it is small but comfortable. Mrs. Conner's children are grown and she works part-time in a camping supplies store not far from where she lives. Throughout our meeting, Mrs. Conner reminisced and reflected on the New Orleans school crisis of 1960. Three of Mrs. Conner's nine children had been enrolled in Frantz School at the time. For Mrs. Conner, what she did was not the result of an ideological stance; or as she put it, "I wasn't a crusader."

The Conners lived a half block from the school. It was their "neighborhood school." Interestingly, the children attended parochial school until 1958, and they transferred to public school because of the cost of parochial school tuition. Like everyone else in New Orleans, Mrs. Conner knew that token integration would begin on November 14. She had no idea which schools would be first to integrate. Her involvement was at home:

> I was always so busy with my family. I was living in a very small world. And I was, I hate to say, a devoted parent. But what can you do? You have to be devoted with nine kids. I wasn't really involved in school activities. I didn't even go to Parent-Teacher Association. I was always pregnant and I was pregnant with the last one at the time. I wasn't aware of what they had planned. I got the impression that they had had a meeting beforehand and that they knew that the school might be the one and that they had decided that they would walk out.

Other whites who took their children out of school have since acknowledged that they had been warned, but they nevertheless decided on a walt-and-see approach. Mrs. Conner conveyed a strong impression that her children would have remained at Frantz in any case. Her voice softened noticeably when she spoke about the common reaction to Ruby entering school: "I never understood everybody's excitement about one little girl."

On the morning of November 14, Mrs. Conner sent her children to school just as she had in the past. Moments later, a television announcement reported that Frantz was being integrated. Shortly thereafter, her telephone began ringing. It would continue to ring into the next academic year. The initial calls came from concerned relatives. As local television stations began live coverage from the school, Mrs. Conner went outside to view the scene from a half block away. As she recalled her emotions at that time, they ranged from disbelief, to her family's good luck, to understanding and even compassion for those whites who left the school and those who heckled.

Mrs. Conner found it difficult to comprehend the attention given the "physical reality" of the event. After all, as she said, "It was only one little girl." She also found it difficult to understand the actions of the crowd. She recalled that the crowd did a lot of "showboating" for the television cameras, and that they did thin out after a few weeks. She was, nevertheless, astounded by the actions and language of the crowd. Phone calls she later received included threats and cursing. The latter became sport for children. Mrs. Conner recalled two experiences with the crowd. She would walk to the corner to meet the children at the end of the school day and there she came face to face with the crowd:

> To hear some of those people! Some who were friendly neighbors the day before it happened made really terrible remarks. One personal remark—of course I was pregnant, I didn't ever keep it a secret. I remember somebody next to me saying, "Is it going to be Black or white?" I thought, "My God, what kind of people are they?"

Sometimes the crowd would drift down to the Conner home and as Mrs. Conner described one such occasion twenty-two years later, her voice still revealed traces of amazement:

> There were a lot of women and they did things that were so unwomanly. We had a house that had a garage below it on one side. Of course, with all the kids we closed it in and made it into a long, big, bedroom. It had a big window in front. I had a young Black girl who would come iron for me. When all this started, I sat down with her and said, "You

don't have to come. You might be in danger if you come. I won't be upset and we will still be friends if you don't want to come." And she said, "Oh no, I'll come." You know that kind of fight. So she would come on her day, and one day we were downstairs making the beds and "the women" came and stood in front of my house. We went to the window and she said, "Look at that one, look at that one." Well, doggone it, the women saw us and they turned their backsides to us and shook their backsides. And she said, "Do you have a camera?" I said that I didn't have any film and she said, "That doesn't matter, pretend we are taking a picture." So I got the camera and the women were doing all kinds of nasty movements.

Mrs. Conner's disbelief extended beyond the crowds—or as she called them, "the women." When the Conner children became the only whites still attending Frantz School there were moments of soul searching. As a Catholic, Mrs. Conner sought out her parish priest for counseling:

I even went to talk to the pastor to see if what I was doing was right. I thought, I'm still doing this, is it right? I know it's right. But am I threatening the kids? Am I putting them in jeopardy? So I talked to him and I came home and thought, What did he say? He did not make any commitment. He did not help me at all. He was like, please, you are tainted, don't come here. I hope no one sees you going out.

Along with soul searching there were times of fear: "We had to push our way through the crowd, and I guess I was hoping nothing would happen." Mrs. Conner was well aware that another mother whose children were in school, Daisy Gabrielle, had been knocked to the ground and spat upon. She was not naive about a possibility of violence; after all, she heard continual threats. Mrs. Conner recalled one threat that brought a second priest to her support. Once a week the Catholic children at Frantz School would march single file from the school to the church for catechism. When the white children were taken out of school many of them also stopped attending catechism. Needless to say, the line had become short but the Conner children continued to attend their religion classes:

One day we got a call from the school. They had received a threat that if the children went to catechism we would all be killed on the way. I had two toddlers at home. The FBI man came to the door with the kids and said, "I'm sorry but this is as far as we can take the kids. You are on your own now." I had cleaned up the two toddlers and myself. I said, "We're going to catechism." I looked down the street and there was a mob at the corner—mostly women. I said, "We are going to go right out of the house and we are going to walk close together." They called the church, too, whoever was doing the calling. When we went around the corner here was this priest. Father Smith. He was the only one in the church who had come to see me. He did it on his own. Here he comes with his robes flowing and two altar boys at his sides. He was coming to meet us and get the kids to catechism. So I was carrying one and dragging the other and he came and took the ones who were going to catechism and he said, "You will be all right?" I said, "Yeah, I'll be." Well, the women travelled the next block down, and everytime I would come to a cross street they would be standing there. But they never did anything.

As Mrs. Conner tells the story, the threats and mobs became almost secondary. The priest was not her only support. Family, a close friend, and the president of Save Our Schools were all supportive. Mrs. Conner recalled the family support:

The family thought, "There goes Margaret again. We've got to continue to love her." They supported me because they loved me, not necessarily because they agreed.

It is important to add that there was daily family contact. Both Mr. and Mrs. Conner's parents phoned daily, and Mrs. Conner visited or spoke frequently with her sister. She also had daily contact with her friend Ann Long. Mrs. Long lived around the corner and had become close friends with Margaret Conner when their children attended a Catholic school. Mrs. Long's children still attended Catholic school, but she understood Mrs. Conner's choice and concurred with it. They helped each other with chores and met daily for tea, a ritual that continued throughout the school year.

One person who agreed strongly with the Conners's position was Mary Sand, the president of Save Our Schools, a white group that supported integration. The organization fought the state legislature's attempts to continue segregation, it monitored media coverage of desegregation, its members drove white children to Frantz School, they lobbied the New Orleans business community for support, and they supplied psychological support for the whites who stayed. Mrs. Conner was "taken" by Mary Sand. Her belief in what Mrs. Conner was doing was so strong that it fortified Mrs. Conner's own convictions.

Occasional help also came from local politicians. The district attorney, Hepburn Many, arranged for an unlisted telephone number. A few judges kept in contact with the family, and Harvard social-psychologist Robert Coles became a frequent visitor in the Conners' home. Mrs. Conner's son Pat, who was a sixth-grader at the time, remembers Dr. Coles in this way:

> I don't remember any psychology talk. He was just an older person that was a friendly guy. I think I knew what he was there for and I think I was always thinking. When is he going to start.

The generous support, though, was only the first phase of what Mrs. Conner referred to as "lucky circumstances." Strong in Mrs. Conner's memory is the anonymity the Conner family retained. That was not the case with all the families who kept their children in school. The Foremans and the Gabrielles became media figures. But the media never caught up with the Conners. Even at the end of the year, when local television covered Pat's sixth-grade graduation (he was the only graduate), the family's faces were never shown. The White Citizens' Council did publish their address and their unlisted phone number, but their faces were never publicized.

> One day I had to walk to go to my obstetrician. I had to catch a bus and "the women" found out that I did that and they were at the bus stop waiting to say things to me. I came around the corner and I saw them down there and I said, "Oh God." But I just kept walking and I walked up and stood right next to them. They didn't even realize it was me. As I got in the bus I waved goodbye. But you see I just went and stood and I didn't do anything. No body language, except, of course, my stomach.

The "lucky circumstances" included more than generosity and anonymity. The other people who continued to send their children to school lived in the Desire Housing Project, an open and accessible collection of buildings. Crowds gathered daily outside the Gabrielle home. Their windows were smashed, and they were subjected to vile language on more than one occasion. The Conners, on the other hand, lived in a single home surrounded by their lawn that served as a symbolic barrier. Evidently, "a man's home is his castle" as long as it is not part of a public housing project.

In addition to the relative security of his home, Mr. Conner also enjoyed job security with Lykes Brothers Shipbuilding, coincidentally one of the first businesses in New Orleans to integrate its work force. Mrs. Conner remembered her husband being called before company officials:

> There was a form of harassment that for us amounted to nothing. They'd call (anonymous callers) and say (to Lykes officials), "Do you realize that you have a man down there who is sending his children to school." Lykes Brothers called my husband in and said, "We don't understand, but we don't interfere." In a way, they reassured him that his job was safe. Of course, other people lost their jobs. So again, we were in a position of advantage.

Compared to other people who continued to send their children to Frantz School, the Conners "were in a position of advantage." Besides being harassed at home, Mr. Gabrielle, who worked for the city, was bothered at work. The seminarians received ultimatums to take their children out of school or join the unemployed. Ruby Bridges's father, the late Alton Bridges, lost his job at a neighborhood service station. The Reverend Foreman, who was subsequently transferred numerous times, took a leave of absence from the Methodist church. Mrs. Conner saw her family as having "lucky circumstances." She understood and sympathized with the plight of other families, Black and white. She experienced similar harassment, but she had been shielded from the worst of it.

Also of interest is the fact that Mrs. Conner showed a great deal of understanding for those who did the harassing—"the women." In her own way she became politically sophisticated.

> On Pauline Street there were all those poor people who were living in the Desire Project. I think that had a lot to do with it. I always felt one of the reasons that they got out in the streets and did what they did was because they didn't have too many people below them. Sometimes you've got to feel like you're top dog, and they didn't have too much. So they wanted to say, "You can't do this to my school. I'll walk out."

Despite her understanding, Mrs. Conner thought that if the parents who removed their children from school had re-enrolled them the next year, both the school and the neighborhood would have been the better for it. Up until 1960, whites and Blacks had lived amicably together in the Ninth Ward. Mrs. Conner felt they could also do so inside the integrated schools. She sympathized with those who left, but as the 1961-62 school year approached, she urged them to return. Their response was at best mixed:

> We went to the principal and we asked for a list of people who had gone to the school so we could write them a personal letter and tell them that everything was fine and ready for their kids to come to school. Well, we mailed the letters and needless to say some of them came back with little postscripts on them. They were still not happy about things. Some of them started coming back.

The new political involvement of the devoted, uninvolved mother continued. She readily admits that she could no longer avoid participation. Keeping her children in school had become a stand whether she wanted it that way or not. She might have remained detached from events, but she had been called upon to act. She spoke on television before the 1961-62 school year:

> Mary Sand called me and asked if I would be on television with the school board. I said, "What can I say, Mary?" She said, "Just be yourself and say what you feel." So I go to the studio and we're all sitting around and here's the district attorney. He's got a stack of papers and I'm sitting there with nothing. I thought, "God, he's all prepared. He looks great." He turned to me and said, "I'm a nervous wreck." [laugh] I still had no idea what I was going to say, but they gave me a cue and I blanked out everybody and just looked at the camera and made a short plea for everybody to come back to school. The guy in the corner was writing something on the board (a cue to stop talking), but God, I didn't have time to read his note. I was trying to concentrate on my next word.

Mrs. Conner also spoke at PTA meetings at schools scheduled to be integrated. She recalled one of those meetings with a great deal of irony. Lusher School, a wealthy uptown school, served an area that included the mansions of the New Orleans elite. PTA members listened to Mrs. Conner, hoping she would provide them with "the answers." She told them to stick together, even as her thoughts wandered back to Frantz School:

> It was nice and I was thinking as I was sitting there that they were all upper class and educated and intelligent. A lot different than some of the parents of some of the kids at Frantz.

Margaret Conner remained involved in the schooling and schools of her children. "A lot different than some of the parents of some of the kids at Frantz" appeared to be an important part of her recollections of the New Orleans school crisis of 1960. The lower economic position of many of the white people who left Frantz School remained prominent in her memories. She understood that those who pulled their children out of the school felt that integration was being "forced" upon them. At the same time, she wished they had stayed because integration was becoming an American reality. Mrs. Conner's parting thought was, "I wish things had worked out better than they have but I'm not surprised that they haven't. All the whites ran, including ourselves because we later left too." She explained that:

We had a really nice house and I liked the immediate neighborhood. I was sorry to leave the school. I didn't want to desert it. On the other hand, I was headed out to the suburbs. My sister lived out in the parish and I had always wanted to live out there—it was called Little Farms. An old house came on the market and we ended up getting it. I hated to move but I wanted to live out that way and my sister had seven kids and I had nine and it was kind of nice. What was really strange was that we just tumbled from one thing into another. We moved out there in the late summer and I decided to try the Catholic schools again. Well, don't you know, that year they decided to integrate that school.

One Who Left and One Who Stayed: Teacher Recollections and Reflections of School Desegregation in New Orleans

On November 14, 1960, as New Orleans began token school integration, the city still viewed itself as uniquely cosmopolitan and tolerant. After all, the trolleys and the library had been integrated without incident. Nevertheless, struggle and conflict accompanied the integration of public schools. The New Orleans schools were the only Louisiana schools open November 14 when two previously all-white elementary schools, McDonogh 19 and Frantz, became integrated. United States marshals escorted three African-American children into McDonogh 19 and one African-American child into Frantz. By midday, parents had removed most of the white children from both schools (Inger, 1969). The subsequent white boycott lasted the entire school year. It was complete at McDonogh 19, while a small number of white children remained at Frantz School the rest of the year. Integration dramatically altered the ethnography of these schools. Prior to November 14, each had enrolled approximately 550 students, employed a principal, a secretary, a janitor, and eighteen teachers. After November 14, African-Americans throughout the city endured verbal and physical harassment as did the few white families who kept their children in Frantz School (Inger, 1969). The teachers at these two schools were greatly affected, and their stories provide valuable insights into school integration in that city.

Surprisingly few studies draw upon the recollections and reflections of teachers regarding school integration in the

United States, and none give teachers an active voice. Meyer Weinberg's (1981) massive bibliography contains 540 citations under the heading "teacher." Of these, only a few relate to teachers's reactions to integration and only one records the recollections and reflections of teachers. The others represent surveys and, although valuable, they provide no individual recollections and reflections per se. (For the one, see Coles, 1964a, pp. 72–73, 90.) This chapter includes two of those missing voices. The first section reviews the literature on teacher recollections and reflections of school integration. The second section presents two case studies on New Orleans teachers, one who left McDonogh 19 and one who stayed at Frantz. The third section draws some conclusions about teacher recollections and reflections on school integration in New Orleans.

Teacher Recollections and Reflections

The literature, to repeat, is sparse. Robert Coles's (1964a) article in the *Saturday Review* pieced together parts of his famous *Children of Crisis* (1964) series. Levinson and Wright (1976) recounted the stories of five teachers from Chicago, Hattiesburg, San Francisco, and Detroit. But only Coles's (1964a) article offers similarities and differences in teacher reactions, pointing to uncertainty, racism, and the disparity between their beliefs and their roles. These concerns were mirrored by New Orleans teachers in 1960. (Some of Coles's teachers are also New Orleanians.) A male teacher in Atlanta told Coles of his uncertainty:

> I almost had to pinch myself that first day when they came down the hall; and when the girl walked into my classroom I have to admit I was as confused as the boys and girls. You could hear a pin drop. In all my years of teaching I've never had a class so quiet. It was real strange the way she'd come in and a kind of stillness came over all of us. Talk about learning; we sure have been getting some (p. 72).

None of Coles's teachers speaks in favor of integration. In spite of that, they grew less and less patient with the white mobs:

> Who can ever forget the looks on those faces? I always thought I was a segregationist, but I never heard such language, and they became so impossible after a while that they belonged in a zoo, not on the

streets. That little nigra child had more dignity than all of them put together—it makes you stop and think (p. 73).

New Orleans teachers related similar experiences. Twenty-five years after the event, in 1985, they felt on reflection that integration's time had certainly come in 1960. By 1985, they sounded more like a number of the teachers Coles interviewed:

> I find myself torn. I never wanted this, but now we have to live with it, and whatever I say at home has nothing to do with what I have to do every day I come to work (p. 72).

A second teacher stated the matter more precisely:

> The crowds outside wanted me to boycott the schools, too; and I was with them, then, to be truthful. I mean I was opposed to desegregation. But I had my job as a teacher, and I just couldn't walk out of the building like that (p. 73).

Similar words were spoken by the teachers in New Orleans. In fact, I found a small number of teachers agreeing with the last of Coles's respondents:

> I just didn't believe it would work. I've known nigras all my life, and I didn't think they would adjust to our schools. I have nothing against them. I just thought their minds weren't like ours (p. 73).

Harry Edwards's autobiography (1980) introduced a like-thinking teacher. An African-American eighth-grade student in 1954 when the Supreme Court ruled on the *Brown* case, Edwards recalled his response:

> I entered Junior high school in 1954, the year of the Supreme Court's first major school desegregation decision. All my teachers seemed to be talking about it—to each other—but, with the exception of one old, Bible-thumping spinster about to retire with almost forty years of teaching behind her, none of them ever discussed the decision in any class that I attended. (And even this old woman's message to us was that "you little darkies aren't ready for integration") (p. 70).

Florence Levinsohn and Benjamin Wright (1976) collected a different set of teacher perceptions, based on the views of both white and Black instructors. Five teachers, Sylvia Fischer of Chicago, Helen Nicholson and Miriam Vance of Hattiesburg, Mississippi, Florence Lewis of San Francisco, and Nellie Brodis of Detroit, reflected on their experiences in desegregated schools. The editors' introduction to their teachers' stories is worth repeating, a statement that accurately describes the frustrations of some of the teachers at McDonogh 19 and Frantz schools in New Orleans:

> It is not particularly astounding to discover, in reading their comments, that these teachers are angry. They are angry at the "system" that has failed to provide them with an atmosphere in which they can use their skills most efficiently. They are, contrary to much received wisdom, deeply concerned about the children they teach. They are passionate in their concern for their schools. They see the center coming apart (p. 173).

Les Scharfenstein, the white teacher who left McDonogh 19, matches this characterization nicely.

The views Levinsohn and Wright recorded offer micro and macro interpretations of the move toward integrated schools. On the one hand, Sylvia Fischer, a veteran white teacher, provided a broad analysis of desegregation in Chicago. Although she was based at an integrated school in the mid-1960s, her reflections focus on school board decisions and her school board's "will to fail." Ironically, the school superintendent she spoke of in Chicago, James Redmond, served as the New Orleans superintendent in 1960, and a "will to fail" fairly reflects the board's attitude toward school desegregation there in 1960.

On the other hand, the Mississippi and San Francisco teachers offer more personal recollections. Helen Nicholson, a veteran African-American teacher at Hattiesburg High School, spoke of the pros and cons of integration:

> Yes, in my opinion, school desegregation is still a good idea for the purpose of providing adequate teaching materials and supplies and for dispelling some of the fallacies usually associated with the races. No, desegregation is not still a good idea from a humanistic point of view (p. 187).

Nicholson's "humanistic" point of view is thoroughly portrayed in Edwards's autobiography. What she referred to is the all-African-American school as a community in itself—as in a family, where everyone knows everyone else and everyone cares about everyone else. In spite of this reality, Edwards opted for integrated schools. He, like Nicholson, did it with a critical eye. There was, he realized, a price to pay, but it was worth paying. "Separate but equal" schools were separate, but they were obviously unequal. Nicholson discussed a second positive aspect of school integration:

> I also feel that school desegregation is still a good idea because it dispels some of the fallacies related to race, and everyone gets an opportunity to see for himself. . . . Blacks have learned that all whites are not smart, and whites have learned that all Blacks are not dumb, there are extremes in all racial groups (p. 188).

Helen Nicholson continued in this vein, avoiding specific problems and dwelling on her support for integrated schools. She believed that challenging education myths and stereotypes would serve African-Americans:

> It is hoped that Black students in the future will be given more positive recognition in areas other than sports, and that Blacks will not make up the greatest percentage of students in special-education and remedial-reading classes (p. 189).

Florence Lewis, a white veteran English teacher at Lowell High School in San Francisco reflecting on her teaching experiences, spoke with deep emotion of America's racism and the consequent resentment African-American students feel. She recalled being hated because of her race:

> I know what it feels like to ask a human being a question and to have him turn away from me and walk down the hall as if I did not exist. The question is not am I big enough to take this acting out of what others have done to him. The question is how long can I take it and teach. The question is not whether I am elite enough to put a stop to elitism but elite enough to say—Look, both of us are wrong if we continue in this fashion (p. 198).

"What others have done to him" is an essential insight if we are to understand Miss Lewis's reaction to school integration. She spent a large portion of her essay discussing the education that Ellis, one of her students, has been cheated out of by racism:

> But what I am trying to make clear is the climate of the sixties—how much injustice the Black kids had suffered, how much they had been left out of a traditionally solid education and certainly the fun of

going to school . . . how necessary desegregation was in order to give
them a chance because they were the dispossessed (p. 198).

Florence Lewis's reflections provide a succinct critical analysis of class, race, and the societal and educational reality in
the United States. She proceeded, however, from a personal
perspective, and the issues she raised remain to be addressed.

One Who Left and One Who Stayed:
Recollections and Reflections

The recollections and reflections of New Orleans teachers re-
semble those of the teachers introduced in the foregoing section. Each teacher's social and cultural situation, as well as
different school realities, however, influenced their memories
and perceptions of school desegregation. Family, religion, class,
race, and geography had an effect on both how teachers responded when their schools were integrated and how they
perceive that event today. The particular school situation is
also important. New Orleans public schools maintained an
astounding student teacher ratio of six-to-one because of the
white boycott. In addition to the boycott, crowds assembled
daily at each school, violence permeated the city, teachers
experienced harassment as they came and left, and their home
telephones rang nightly with obscenities and threats. Against
this backdrop we begin to explore the recollections and reflections of two teachers: Les Scharfenstein and Josie Ritter.

Les Scharfenstein
I interviewed Les Scharfenstein in his office at the St. Bernard
Parish school board near New Orleans. Scharfenstein had been
director of food services in that district for ten years but was a
teacher at the time of the boycott. The district adjoins Orleans
Parish and actually abetted the white boycott at McDonogh 19
and Frantz when Leander Perez, Attorney General of Plaquemines Parish and a racist power broker in southern Louisiana,
arranged for the white children from Orleans Parish to be accepted in St. Bernard. In essence, St. Bernard schools became
one of two educational options for white children, the other
being a segregationist academy Perez also supported.

Scharfenstein described the initial confusion the order to integrate the public schools caused, his day-to-day experiences as a teacher in a boycotted school, his hope that white children would return, his empathy for white parents, his contempt for the integration process, and his eventual departure from McDonogh 19. Scharfenstein's confusion was unlike the confusion at Frantz School. Jack Stewart, McDonogh 19's principal, had notified the faculty about preparations for integrating the school prior to the morning of November 14. Scharfenstein and the rest of the faculty had immediate duties:

> I was a sixth grade teacher at the time and we arrived at school to find people on the neutral ground and policemen on horseback. The principal called us together to get things organized. In fact he even stationed us at each of the entrances so only the children could enter. We would not allow the parents to enter the school but we assured them that their children would be all right.

Despite the preparations by midday all of the white children had been removed by their parents from McDonogh 19, and the school accommodated only three six-year-old African-American girls for the rest of the school year. The recollections of the school's principal, Jack Stewart, included praise for the faculty, who vainly tried to follow a traditional school day:

> The teachers went out of their way to see that they got good instruction. We still made the three of them file in a row to come down the steps. You see that's what school's about to a little child.

But, for Scharfenstein, this situation generated a great deal of frustration. His memories stress the lack of teaching:

> In the meantime we were left with no children to teach from early November. By Christmas time several of us were getting a little leery of doing busy work. We became engaged in a curriculum study but it was really busy work and we knew it and everyone else knew it.

Scharfenstein and the other teachers hoped that the white children would return. But by Christmas, they realized that the white parents had found alternatives for their children, enrolling them in either the Ninth Ward Cooperative School or in the St. Bernard schools. Scharfenstein empathized with their choice:

> I spoke to a few people. I could understand their position. For a parent to have sent their children back to that school they might have been creating some problems for themselves in their own neighborhood. I can understand why they might not have done it, because of the pressure that was being brought to bear by their peers, by the people in their community. I certainly would not have advised them to do something that would have created a problem for them.

The local papers, the *Times Picayune* and the *States Item*, reported the systematic harassment of two families, the Foremans and the Gabrielles. Each family met confrontation on the way to school, in the workplace, and at home; each was finally frightened away from Frantz School.

Just as Scharfenstein viewed school integration as creating a dilemma for white parents, he felt that the white parents understood the dilemma of McDonogh 19 teachers:

> Those who knew us as faculty members knew that we were in the same position that they were in. We were having something forced on us that we really had no choice in. I don't think they held it against us personally. I think they understood our position as we understood theirs.

Stewart's recollections matched Scharfenstein's:

> There was little harassment of any of our faculty. Now I understand at the other school it was somewhat different. Our teachers never stopped parking their cars right out on the street. It was almost as if the community separated the faculty of the school from whatever else was going on. I think it was a credit to the teachers who were there. We could see them on the streets in the evening and they would talk about everything and anything. They did not come across to us with any animosity.

The word "force" appeared often in the reflections of both men. Stewart firmly stated that integration's time had definitely come by 1960. Scharfenstein made no definitive statement about the political issue itself, but he said that he had nothing against teaching Black children. (That seems now like an absurd statement, but it passed for tolerance in 1960.) Although Scharfenstein seemed less than insightful in his critique of New Orleans school integration, he did resent the procedures:

> Force—this was the objection of most of the people. I think that integration might have been done differently. If they just had said we have the same assignments for all children, Black and white, as we had before. However, the doors of all schools are open to any student that wants to transfer to another school. I think this is really what Black people wanted at the time.

Scharfenstein's analysis ignores the continuing African-American struggle in New Orleans and throughout the nation for civil rights. In fact, his emphasis on force changed the issue— that is, it implied that the imposition of the federal government represented a greater evil than the white racism endemic in New Orleans, not to say most of American society. One could point out that the same people who resisted federal intervention in civil rights matters never resisted federal, state, or local white racism. Not that New Orleans school integration proceeded in the most humanistic or efficient manner possible. Recall that two schools in affluent areas had volunteered to integrate, but the school board, which consistently made bad choices, selected two other schools, both in lower and lower-middle-class neighborhoods. The Board appeared to condone integration only for poor whites and poor Blacks. Thus, Scharfenstein's (and others') references to integration as "force" might help one understand the behavior of the white community in opposition to integration, but it should not be used as justification—such actions were illegitimate.

Although Scharfenstein claimed he did not mind teaching African-American children and his reasons for leaving McDonogh 19 differed from those of the boycotting white families, his departure calls for further scrutiny. First, listen to his reflections on his move from McDonogh 19 to St. Bernard Parish's Arabi Elementary School:

> We had only those three children in the school. There really wasn't much for us. We reported to school every day. We met together. We didn't know what the future held. We didn't know what the response of parents would be. We did not know whether or not the children would return to school. I think we held out hope that they would. We expected that they would, but they didn't because other provisions

were made. By Christmas of that year we began to wonder if there wasn't some possibility to be transferred to another school . . . that is as teachers. Many of us felt we'd like to get back to teaching. I went to the personnel office. I spoke to the personnel director and explained how I felt. He responded that the board's hands were tied. There was nothing they could do but keep us there. They had to maintain a faculty. My reply was that mine weren't. I came down to St. Bernard and spoke to the Superintendent, and sure enough there was an opening. In early January I began teaching in St. Bernard. I became a sixth grade teacher at Arabi Elementary School. As I said, for me it turned out to be probably the best thing that ever happened.

While for Scharfenstein, the integration of McDonogh 19 and his consequent departure "turned out to be probably the best thing that ever happened," he knew well he was teaching many of the same children at Arabi he had taught before at McDonogh 19. Still he did not acknowledge the white boycott as a precondition of his being hired in St. Bernard. He did recollect being welcomed by the white children and their families:

They were glad to see me come down there, although they might have misinterpreted my motives. When I came to Arabi, I was kind of cheered. Anyone who asked me, I explained that I was there because I wanted to teach. I felt good about being back in the classroom. I felt good about the move. It didn't take me long to like the idea of teaching down here.

Scharfenstein appeared never to have anguished over or analyzed his decision. His words are nevertheless important, precisely because they reveal no analysis of the integrated school situation. His departure seemed to be his own individual choice, but he ignored the fact that the job at Arabi materialized because of the boycott of the newly integrated school. Although Scharfenstein had no qualms about teaching African-American children, his move to St. Bernard became possible only because the white people at McDonogh 19 refused to allow their children to attend an integrated school and transferred them into a nearby all-white system.

One cannot doubt Scharfenstein's desire to teach, but the issue went beyond his need for personal satisfaction. Teachers at both integrated schools were offered alternative positions at the Ninth Ward Cooperative School, yet only one teacher at each school failed to complete the school year. True, Les Scharfenstein and the other teachers at McDonogh 19 experienced pressure and stress. On the other hand, like it or not, his departure, just like the white families' boycott, made a political statement about the perceived importance of school integration in New Orleans in 1960. Scharfenstein and the whites who left might have been well instructed by Margaret Conner, the mother of one of the two white families who kept their children in Frantz whom we met in the preceding chapter. She spoke of the reaction to Ruby Bridges, the Black child who enrolled in Frantz: "I never understood everyone's excitement about one little girl."

Josie Ritter

Josie Ritter's memories of school desegregation struck a far different note. She seemed more descriptive, and she displayed a strong sense of altruism. At the time of the school crisis, Mrs. Ritter had been a white teacher at Frantz School for seven years. When we met in 1982, she showed me pictures of the children playing in the schoolyard at Frantz School. Photos from 1960 show Ruby Bridges, the one Black child who integrated the school, playing with the few white children who still attended Frantz. Although Mrs. Ritter told me that she had not looked at the pictures in years, she took obvious delight in the smiles on the children's faces. At that time, a smile was a rarity at Frantz School. My interviews with Josie Ritter covered a number of themes: her initial reaction; the reaction of her principal (a woman, Estelle Barkemeyer, and quite a different sort of person from Jack Stewart); the reactions of the white parents; the daily reality at the school; the reactions of family, friends, and other teachers; and Mrs. Ritter's disappointment in the school board.

Josie Ritter clearly liked Frantz School and the community. She remembered the faculty being honored by the school's PTA just three days before it was integrated: "The parents' club had a celebration for us. They brought all different kinds of pies and cakes and they gave each of us a gift."

That same day the principal was informed that Frantz would be integrated. Unlike Mr. Stewart, Mrs. Barkemeyer kept the news to herself. Mrs. Ritter knew that school integration would begin on November 14, but she did not expect Frantz to be one of the integrated schools. She drove to work that morning with Earlene Schubert, a fellow teacher, and she recalled their surprise:

> When we turned the corner to the school we saw one of the TV stations shooting film. I'll never forget, she said, "Son of a bitch, we're the ones that are integrating." We were shocked. We could not park near the school so we went down the block. As we walked to the school the newscaster wanted a statement. We asked them what was going on and they told us that Frantz had been chosen to be integrated. Well, we were absolutely shocked, we didn't know what to do.

Mrs. Ritter recollected confusion. The white children were already at the school; Ruby Bridges would not arrive until later in the morning. Rumors spread quickly and the school lacked a plan and appeared to lack leadership. Mrs. Barkemeyer was nowhere to be found. But one of the parents who kept her children in Frantz School throughout the school year, Mrs. Chandler, remembered Mrs. Barkemeyer telling white parents that the school was open under federal order and that they were welcome to take their children home. She then asked all the parents to leave. Mrs. Chandler never once saw Mrs. Barkemeyer during the rest of the year.

Josie Ritter also recalled the invisible principal: "Barkemeyer, we did not see her. She disappeared. She did not know her faculty, and we did not know her: she was a stranger." A second recollection is even more telling:

> Her brother and Mr. Moorehouse, a representative from the Board of Education, one on each arm would carry her into the school each morning. She wouldn't come in. I think she was scared, because when the police or anybody would come into the building she would say she was Miss Smith. She had her ranking teacher deal with them. She would hide.

Mrs. Ritter's memories might seem somewhat dramatic, but other teachers as well as the two white mothers whose children remained at Frantz considered Mrs. Barkemeyer a virtual phantom. Moreover, her absence promoted confusion and exacerbated the already difficult transition. Many of the faculty members had served the school for several comfortable years and feared the change. Mrs. Ritter believed that the principal who had retired the year before, a veteran both of the school and the community, would have provided enough leadership to encourage the faculty and quash the white boycott:

> She was a very straight-backed woman. She would have gone down those front steps and told those people to go home and leave her and the kids alone. There would not have been a boycott.

But, she had retired; thus, the teachers lacked support and the white parents removed their children.

As at McDonogh 19, one of the teachers joined the boycott. Actually, she acted before Ruby Bridges even arrived at the school and before the parents' boycott began. As the first-grade teacher, she was scheduled to teach Ruby, and in some ways, her refusal to carry out her assignment brought the other teachers together and gave them the strength to persevere. Mrs. Ritter remembered the teachers' discussion on the morning of November 14:

> Everybody was talking about it. She lived in the neighborhood and she was at her house screaming and crying. She said that she couldn't do it, and she never did come. The other teachers who lived in the neighborhood came in and everyone signed in except her.

Although unsure of precisely what they should be doing, the teachers seemed at first disconcerted by the extreme reaction of their colleague. They also appeared shocked by the community's reaction. The same community members who had honored them just three days earlier removed their children before Ruby even entered the school:

> The parents all came and they were hauling their children out. They said they weren't going to let their children be at school with a nigger. You know, that kind of talk.

Mrs. Ritter recalls the crowd growing outside the school and reacting vocally when the federal marshals escorted Ruby into the school. She offered this insight into their reaction: "The federal marshals brought her in the front door, and that is what really infuriated the white people."

In retrospect, the initial crowd reaction seems mild considering what would happen in the days to come. The white families who kept their children in Frantz were unmercifully ha-

rassed. The teachers, Mrs. Ritter included, also felt antago-
nism; they were confronted face-to-face by the whites who left
the school, and they were victimized nightly by obscene telephone calls. Mrs. Ritter recalled some of her encounters with
parents:

> There was one father whose child had lost a library book. They had
> paid for the book, but then the book was found at the school. The
> family made no attempt to get their money back. After the school was
> integrated the father came in and asked for his money back. What
> did he say to me? We were all "nigger lovers" and he didn't care if he
> had his money back before, but now he wanted his money back.

It would, however, be unfair to portray the entire neighborhood as aligned against the faculty. Mrs. Ritter did receive
supportive calls from the parents of some of her ex-students.
Some said they wanted to keep their children in Frantz School,
but the community pressure was just too great and they were
afraid. At the opposite extreme, the crowds that gathered outside of Frantz often spat upon the teachers and the white parents whose children remained in school:

> We no longer parked our cars on the street. We had to park in the
> school yard, or they would spit at us or damage our cars. The police
> had to escort us out of the neighborhood.

Josie Ritter also remembered the phone calls:

> We had to have our phone changed to a silent number. Oh, they
> would call, and what they wouldn't call me! It was horrible. There we
> were, the people they had honored just three days before, and they
> were saying that we should leave. But the words they used!

Mrs. Ritter and her family quickly felt the stress. Her supportive husband encountered confrontation with his acquaint-
ances and workmates. Mrs. Ritter expressed disappointment
in the community's reaction to her and her fellow teachers.
She sadly remembered the whites who boycotted because of
pressure and fear rather than intense racism. One parent told
her, "I can't send them back, Josie, I just can't do it. Your neigh-
bors won't talk to you." Another parent spoke similar words,
"I won't let my little girl go to Frantz and be subject to those
people [crowds]. Not that I care if she goes to school with a

Black child, but I know what happens to the white kids on the way to school." Josie Ritter summed up her reflections on the Frantz School parents in this statement:

> The main thing that I would say was that the people that honored us turned on us so quickly. It's a shame that the people couldn't have accepted it. I never dreamed that these people would all pull their children out of school. Even after we knew we were integrated we were going to have school.

Because of the white boycott, Frantz could not function as a school in the traditional sense. By the end of the year, its student body included Ruby Bridges, the four Conner children, and the two Chandler girls. A new first-grade teacher, Barbara Henry, served as Ruby's teacher, but the other teachers split their duties. In addition to the stress of the crowds and the community, the teachers also suffered the daily uncertainties in the school. With no leadership, they no longer worked at the same school they had known, and they wondered whether they were really teaching?

Mrs. Ritter spoke of the frustrations of being idle. With so few children, teachers had a great deal of free time, and she became especially upset when teachers from other schools spoke cynically of teachers at Frantz and McDonogh 19 receiving their pay for nothing. (Actually, the state of Louisiana cut funding for both schools in early December.) A missed paycheck caused teacher morale to plummet. Although Mrs. Ritter chose not to elaborate on her salary, Jack Stewart offered these recollections:

> One day I was downtown, and I got back to the building and I knew something was wrong. Everybody was in their own room. You could just feel it. When you've got three kids, that's not typical. You know the faculty had a blowup. I just got on the horn and said, "I want to see you all when school lets out."
>
> I just went around the table and apparently a few guys on the faculty were really hurting for money. I said, "Alright, what do you want to do? Do you want to walk out?" After we chatted for awhile, we all decided we didn't know what to do, so we were going to do nothing. We just came back the next day.

In spite of tensions like these, the teachers tried to lift the morale of one another and of the children. Mrs. Ritter spoke with fond memories of teachers, police, and United States marshals dancing and singing at the school's Christmas party. When I mentioned that Mrs. Conner told me one of her daughters learned to play the piano that year, she described the teaching that went on at the school:

> We did everything. We had crocheting. We had art work for them. Those children got the best education. There were two third grade teachers and one third grade child. She and I taught in the morning and she taught in the afternoon. We had all the regular subjects and so much more. We had programs and parties for Christmas and Easter. We made a lot of things go on for them. It was for us, too.

As much as they tried, 1960-61 stretched into a long and frustrating school year. The white children did not return and, although the faculty tried to make the best of it, they were happy to see the year come to an end.

Josie Ritter's family and friends also played important roles in the integration initiative. Mr Ritter worked as a foreman at an integrated utility company. He supported Josie and had no qualms about her teaching at Frantz. Most of the family friends also supported her, but a few disagreed. Some broke off their friendship and others got in their digs (and still do): "Josie, you still a 'nigger lover'? like that. And I say, 'Yes!'"

Although by 1960 Josie Ritter had concluded it was time for the schools of New Orleans to integrate, she expressed concern about the way the change came about. In that sense, she agreed with Les Scharfenstein. She considered both schools unfortunate choices for integration. She did not dwell on "force" or the evils of the federal government, like Scharfenstein. Instead, she named a half dozen schools that she thought could have been integrated with less struggle and resistance.

Mrs. Ritter's memories, deeply personal, fairly reflect her values and personality. I gained further insight into Josie Ritter hearing her describe how her own daughter's school was later integrated:

> I was teaching and I was called to my daughter's school the day they integrated. The mothers were outside and they said that they didn't want their children going to school with Blacks. I told them that they were acting foolish. I said that I had been through this and that my

daughter was staying right in that school where she belonged. One of the teachers was outside with the mothers, and she was asking what she should do. I told her that she should go back into the school and teach because that was what she was supposed to be doing whether the kids were Black or white.

Conclusion

The reactions of the teachers to school integration obviously varied in New Orleans, and neither Les Scharfenstein nor Josie Ritter offer extreme examples. He was hardly an arch-segregationist and she was hardly a grassroots integrationist. But their stories provide personal perspectives of school integration. Neither appeared to carry the event with them heavily 23 years later. Mrs. Ritter told me that she seldom thinks of that time— only when people like me ask her about it. Mr. Scharfenstein still views the event as a stroke of good luck. He considered his move to St. Bernard as completely separate from the white parents moving their children to St. Bernard to avoid integration. Although Josie Ritter generally favored integration, she did not do so within the framework of any active resistance to the organizational and psychological white racism that persists in New Orleans. Both teachers' stories feature more recollection than reflection. How they experienced the event— how it worked on them and how they reacted to or worked on it—was more important than race and white racism as a social reality. Their stories can, therefore, help one to understand why *de facto* school segregation remains a reality in their city.

Very few teachers exist—or few of anyone else, for that matter—whose reactions to the beginnings of school integration are as sensitive as those of that San Francisco teacher, Florence Lewis. She has the wonderful ability to connect the societal and educational class disparity and white racism with how it affects real people. While Les Scharfenstein and Josie Ritter addressed white racism or their students only in passing, Miss Lewis talked continually about her relationship to her students, especially those students who have been consistently ignored and disenfranchised. Although we occasionally find others like Miss Lewis, most of us dwell more upon how we are personally affected, and we tend to be more than willing to confuse our personal troubles with societal issues. This perspective leads us to ignore class disparity and racism and instead to "blame the victim." True enough, if the teachers at McDonogh 19 or Frantz schools had been more like Miss Lewis, the school crisis might still have occurred. But, without more teachers like Miss Lewis, true school and social integration are impossible.

Chapter 9

The New Orleans School Crisis of 1960: The Blacks Who Integrated

On November 14, 1960, the city of New Orleans initiated token desegregation of its schools, an event still referred to acidly as "the New Orleans school crisis." The Louisiana Advisory Committee to the United States Commission for Civil Rights published a chronology of the events, and Morton Inger wrote *Politics and Reality in an American City*, a political history of the crisis. This chapter chronicles the stories of the Black families whose children integrated the two schools, and they are a crucial element of the desegregation story in New Orleans.

As in the determination of the two schools which was discussed in preceding chapters, the selection of the Black children invited to enroll in white schools proceeded "scientifically." The school board's computer considered these eighteen factors:

(1) nearness of the school to the child's home,
(2) parents' reasons,
(3) available room and teaching capacity of the schools,
(4) transportation,
(5) scholastic aptitude scores,
(6) intelligence or ability test scores,
(7) results of achievement tests,
(8) effects of new pupils on the program,
(9) suitability of curricula for pupils,
(10) pupil's academic preparation,
(11) psychological qualification for the school,

(12)   effect on other students' academic progress,
(13)   effect upon academic standards,
(14)   psychological effects on pupil,
(15)   home environment,
(16)   pupil's relationship with teachers and classmates,
(17)   interests of the pupil, and
(18)   possibility of threat or friction (Crain, 1969, pp. 260–261).

One hundred and thirty-six Black children volunteered to transfer but only five met the computer's programmed criteria. All five selected were girls, gender being absent from the eighteen criteria even though interrelated attitudes on sex and race were very much a part of the desegregation issue in southern Louisiana. As soon as the schools were integrated in New Orleans, classes were segregated by sex, while two adjoining school districts ended their unisex classrooms in the 1980s. The relationship between sex and white racism in the United States extends far beyond the scope of this discussion, but let us not forget that it is very strong.

The five Black children selected to attend McDonogh 19 and Frantz were notified by telegram on Sunday, November 13. One family declined the offer. Three children—Tessie Prevost, Leona Tate, and Gail Etiene—enrolled in McDonogh 19. Ruby Bridges went to Frantz. *Newsweek* described the scene as Ruby entered Frantz School for the first time:

> Her mother had spent hours that morning dressing her, primping her. When she stepped from the Federal marshals' closed sedan, she was a symphony in white and blue. She wore a snow-white dress and a snow-white knit sweater, bright blue stockings, and glossy new shoes. She was frightened, obviously, and she clutched her mother, a slender woman, in a light blue sweater and dark blue plaid skirt, who obviously was frightened too. Hand in hand, they walked up the steps of the William Frantz school. Across the street, a crowd gathered and, as they started up the steps, the crowd let out a long, heartfelt boo. They walked slowly, and every step was punctuated by yelling and insults. The little girl turned from her mother to look at the crowd, and then she disappeared into the school (*Newsweek*, Nov. 28, 1960, p. 19).

By midday, parents had removed a great number of white children from McDonogh 19 and prepared to boycott the school for the entire school year. In the end, three children, eighteen teachers, the principal, the cook, and the janitor constituted the total makeup of McDonogh 19 school. The number of white children at Frantz varied between four and twenty for the rest of that year.

Shortly after the start of desegregation, Robert Coles presented portraits of the Bridges and Prevost families in *Children of Crisis*. Coles spent time with both families throughout 1961.

The Bridges

The Bridges had come to New Orleans from Mississippi in 1955. Mr. Bridges had learned auto mechanics in the Marines and was employed at a service station in 1960. Like many of the white fathers fired from their jobs for keeping their children in Frantz School, Alton Bridges was fired for sending his Black daughter. He was soon hired, though, by a Black service station owner. Coles (1964) described him when he was unemployed:

> He tended to be morose at home. He sat looking at the television, or he sat on the front steps of the house carving a piece of wood, throwing it away, hurling the knife at the house's wood, then fetching a new branch to peel, cut and again discard. He also suffered a loss of appetite (pp. 48–49).

According to Coles, Bridges was overwhelmed that his daughter's attendance at an integrated school accounted for his dismissal. The Bridges family was neither radical nor ideological. In fact, Alton Bridges had no idea Ruby would be the only Black child at Frantz School: "We agreed to sign for Ruby to go to the white school because we thought it was for all the colored to do," he stated. "We never thought Ruby would be alone" (p. 75). Coles viewed the Bridges family as remarkably average. Mr. Bridges believed in hard work and Mrs. Bridges worked conscientiously to raise their family, which included Ruby, her two younger sisters, and a younger brother. At six, Ruby seemed perfectly normal:

> Ruby, then was learning to be a good girl, a rather conventional task for one of her age. Her envies, her feelings of rivalry toward others in her family, are not unusual. She is a girl of sound mind and body, a

lively, rather perceptive child whose drawings and frolic show imagination even as they indicate the normal anxieties and fears of a growing child. Were it not for the intersection of her childhood with a
moment of our country's history, her difficulties would not be under
discussion (p. 81).

This is not to say that Ruby went unaffected by the event. The
most famous—notorious, really—story involves her decision to
stop eating when a woman in the mob outside of the school
threatened her each day with poisoning: "And that one lady
tells me every morning I'm getting poisoned soon, when she
can fix it" (p. 77). At the time Ruby, as a six-year-old, could
hardly comprehend that her skin color could be so important.
Later as a young woman with her own family she still felt the
effects of being one of the first four to integrate. She has ac-
ceded to her husband's wishes and no longer gives lengthy
interviews, but Ruby is an intelligent and vital woman. Nevertheless, one senses she feels cheated by the event. It is not that
she regrets having been chosen, but rather that she continues
to feel—or remember vividly—the strain. Others like Coles came
to interview her. Scholarships were promised, and reporters
became a part of everyday life. But as time passed, Ruby found
herself alone. Coles and the media were gone, and the scholarships never materialized. Only the burden remained. Ruby
remains friendly and warm, but when one speaks with her it is
obvious that she carries a great weight. Being one of the first
four is constantly with her. (It should be noted that in the last
year Ruby Bridges has coauthored a children's book with Robert Coles. She is presently appearing on television interviews
where she discusses her experiences during school integration
as well as her current work as a school–community liaison at
Frantz School, which is currently an all-Black school.)

The Prevosts

Robert Coles also studied the Prevost family (1964), which then
lived and still lives together in a mini-complex. Actually, they
own adjoining houses fenced in together, more like a family
compound. In one house lives Tessie, her sister, and her parents. Next door is her grandmother. Coles described Tessie's
dad as a college graduate who worked at the post office in
1960:

> He [Prevost] is a college graduate. He speaks excellent English. He
> reads widely in magazines and paperbacks, particularly on world af-
> fairs and recent history. He works in the post office sorting letters all
> day. His mother said he wanted to be a lawyer, but getting him through
> college taxed her to the point of exhaustion (p. 89).

Not everyone at the post office was kind to Mr. Prevost, but no
one threatened his job. Ironically, he sorted much of the hate
mail addressed to his daughter. In Coles's analysis of the
Prevosts, he devoted more time to Tessie, her grandmother,
and her mother than to Mr. Prevost, whom Coles found to be a
quiet man. Twenty-four years later Prevost still refused to
discuss the school crisis, but he once told Tessie he did not
believe that a great deal resulted from their sacrifices. New
Orleans schools remain segregated and white racism is, in
Prevost's view, very much an American reality. Tessie's younger
sister still attends a largely segregated school.

Both Tessie and her grandmother, Dora Prevost, however,
think their sacrifice was worth its cost. Neither of them sees
the present reality as harshly as Mr. Prevost. Tessie's mother
stands somewhere between the two perspectives. Coles found
the stress from the crowds hardest on her at the time:

> She had wanted her daughter to go to a desegregated school, but she
> also acknowledged that she worried about the strain of it upon both
> her daughter and herself. "The truth is," she said quietly on a day
> after talking about how she felt when she answered abuse with silence,
> "I might have taken Tessie out, returned her to a Negro school. I held
> firm because my husband held firm, and we both held firm because
> of Tessie's grandmother. My husband and I were angry and scared,
> but she never gets scared, and if she gets angry only she knows it"
> (p. 90).

During my meetings with Tessie and her grandmother at
the complex, Mr. Prevost was usually home but always declined
to be interviewed. When I spoke with Tessie and her grandmother, religious music played softly in the background. Dora
Prevost mentioned being a Christian throughout her discussion of Tessie and desegregation. She also spoke to Coles about
her prayers:

> That night I said my prayers, just as I have for over sixty years, but I
> added something. I said, "Lord, you have started giving New Orleans
> your attention, at last. The whites are screaming at Tessie and me, but
> that's because they know you are watching; and [that they] will be

punished soon, now that You've decided to take a hand in our lives here"' (p. 86).

In many ways Tessie's grandmother was the strength of the Prevost family. She absorbed much of the family's abuse and always answered it with "Christian dignity." She acknowledged the family's suffering, but she always returned to two points when I interviewed her: the authority of the Bible and the importance of integration: "I'm a Christian. My Bible doesn't have segregation in it. Christ is for all. For the life of me, I don't understand why the white people hate the Black people so."

Dora Prevost did not really expect the violent white reaction. She did not anticipate having to remove the phone from the hook because of harassing and obscene phone calls. She would answer them with both wit and decency, but she certainly did not relish the experience: "'You better get that nigger grandchild out of the school,' they'd say, and I'd say, 'Oh, aren't you ashamed, does your preacher know you are calling me?'"

Dora Prevost's analysis of the family's suffering is worth noting: "Her dad just about pulled her out. It would have put integration back ten years. We suffered because she suffered and she suffered for something she didn't understand." Twenty-four years later, despite the suffering, Dora Prevost believes that it was worth it, and she would have her granddaughter do it again:

> I think it was worthwhile. I didn't think it would be all we went through. I would do it again because of the results. Something had to break. Something had to give because we're all human beings. May President Kennedy rest in his grave. When she was abused I told her daddy that somebody has to go through it. Until this day I wonder why it couldn't have just come together. Why did they fight so hard from keeping the colored and white from going to school together? I never will be able to understand that.

Although she is much less certain than her grandmother about the issues of race and education in the United States, Tessie agreed that she would go through the experience again. She had memories of abuse (much of it two years later at a different integrated school), but most of her memories revolve around the excitement. Like Ruby, five-year-old Tessie found the issues to be abstract: "She didn't know what was going on and asked, "Grandma, what are those people out there making all that noise for?" Tessie's memories of the first days include anger at her mother. Seeing the noisy crowd, she remembered thinking Mardi Gras had come early and not understanding why she, Gail, and Leona had to go to school at all. Tessie later learned the difference: "I didn't look the people in the eye. I didn't know why, but I didn't want to look at them."

When I interviewed Tessie much of her memory centered on the attention she received from her teachers (the teacher-student ratio being six to one) and from the media. Tessie enjoyed seeing herself on television and in the newspaper. She also enjoyed telling me about her Aunt Bess who called daily from Washington to tell Tessie she had seen her on television. Needless to say, Aunt Bess did not speak with Tessie about her fear and concern. Finally, Tessie enjoyed the encouraging mail that came from all over the world. She spoke to me of letters from a classroom of first-generation immigrants from Lynn, Massachusetts, a woman from Denver, and a man from Belgium as if they had arrived yesterday. Hate letters also came, but her parents intercepted them.

Tessie went through integrated schools and finally attended the University of Southwestern Louisiana. When I visited she was working at the telephone company, as were Gail and Leona (they had all secured their jobs separately). She said she was not in the least affected, and yet this unique event obviously remains a part of her life.

The Tates

The third child to integrate the New Orleans schools was Leona Tate, and when I interviewed Leona it invariably became a family occasion. Her parents, her husband, and her children usually gathered as we sat at the dining room table, my tape recorder as the centerpiece. The music of children playing replaced the religious music at the Prevosts. Unlike Mr. Prevost, Mr. Tate, as well as his wife and daughter, were more than willing to discuss their experiences. Mr. Tate had worked for years on ships. In fact, he had worked at Delta, the first shipyard in New Orleans to integrate its work force. In 1960, he was a self-employed mechanic. Mr. Tate had found the decision to send Leona to an integrated school easy. Leona had the qualifications, so she went to McDonogh 19. It was as simple as that. Also, as with Tessie, Gail, and Ruby, McDonogh 19 and Frantz were much closer than the segregated schools they attended.

Leona's father left the final school decisions to his wife. He did not appear to be a passive man, but he considered schooling to be his wife's responsibility. He also thought the authorities (police and U.S. marshals) would protect the family. On the other hand, he was hardly naive about the situation: "All I was interested in at the time was that she would get to school safe. Some crackpot could take a shot and harm her. That was my only worry." Mr. Tate also had compassion for Ruby's father who was fired from his job. But Leona's attendance at an integrated school never affected Mr. Tate's work. His white clientele apparently never knew that the Tate family was one of the four pursuing integration:

> I was doing work for a white guy and he didn't know who he was talking to. He said, "So you see what is going on. They're paying those colored people to do that." I listened and thought nobody had ever paid me. Until the day he died he didn't know who I was. He was good to me. He paid me well and treated me well.

Other white people also concluded that the Blacks had been paid off. Mr. Tate spoke to that issue:

> Oh, there were promises. We were promised a college trust fund—never saw it. Archie Moore fought a fight in town and said he was donating his purse to the little girls—never saw it. The only thing Leona received was a hundred dollar bond from Eleanor Roosevelt.

As anonymous as Mr. Tate managed to remain, he enjoyed the attention. He liked getting a letter from Eleanor Roosevelt. He enjoyed having the police chief visit the family home. He particularly enjoyed the visit of Justice Thurgood Marshall, at the time chief counsel for the NAACP:

> It was a Sunday morning. He got out of a car and I recognized him. I was working on an old Buick. I was tuning it up. He stood there and looked and said that he hadn't seen one of those running in a long time.

I found Mr. Tate a warm and gracious man, and yet somewhat blasé about the school crisis. Enrolling Leona had not involved a great deal of contemplation, and there seemed to have been little reflection on the event in the intervening twenty-four years. It was just something the Tates had done—no different from the events that preceded it or those that followed. Not that Mr. Tate was disinterested, his recollections were clear and lively. But so are his memories of his years on the high seas and the years in his backyard garage.

Leona's mother is more strident than her father, and her memories of Leona juxtaposed with the mobs at McDonogh 19 are far more vivid than Mr. Tate's. Many of her friends advised against sending Leona to McDonogh 19. In response, she echoed her husband: "She qualified—she goes." Mrs. Tate recalled Thurgood Marshall encouraging her to continue to send Leona: "I asked him if we should keep with it and he told me, 'Yes, don't be afraid.'" Mrs. Tate escorted Leona on the first day:

> She and I were the first two in the school door. They were hollering that they didn't want their children to go to school. There was one white woman who said that she wanted her child to go. She said these little girls is nice. But the rest didn't want theirs to go.

The mobs remained at the schools, and Mrs. Tate remembered them well. There was some harassment, but she met it head on. Crowds formed outside her house, and "I opened the door wide and I said, 'If you go to your house and do your work you wouldn't have time for all this worry.'" Leona's family who lived in Plaquemines Parish, an area south of New Orleans known for its racist politics, were actually threatened at the time:

> This guy attacked my daddy and he told my dad he was coming up here to make him pull me out of school. I told my daddy just leave him come. If he put one foot on the step someone was going to have to put the other one cause I was goin' to blow him down.

Mr. Tate actually prepared for the man's arrival, but he never came.

The Tates had no qualms about the school. They felt generally secure and they trusted the police and teachers. Most of

Mrs. Tate's bad memories, like those of the Prevosts, came two years later in a different integrated school. Her words best sum up her feelings of being one of the first four families:

> I didn't have no bad feeling about it. I'm not prejudiced because of it, no. If they'd have kept pursuing it the way they said they would it would have been a whole lot different. I think maybe it would be better for kids today. But they just dropped it all of a sudden.

Leona herself remembered the 1960-61 school year as much like other years: "School was the same, only there were only three of us." Interestingly enough, when I spoke with Jack Stewart, the principal of McDonogh 19 during the school crisis, he stressed the conscious effort to proceed normally:

> We still made the three of them file in a row to come down the steps. You see that's what school is about to a little child. Just because there are only three you're still going to do it like it's school because there's going to be a day when there's going to be school again with a lot of kids. You can't be different.

Leona remembered being with Tessie and Gail, and she recalled the teachers being "nice." For Leona the memories that stand out are, in fact, the "nice" ones—like the letters of encouragement from all over the world. One person who stood out in her mind was a Mr. Lewis from Chicago, who sent Leona small gifts. Another recollection was of strangers throwing her a party in a Virginia hotel because they recognized her from television accounts of the school crisis. Leona also had fond memories of Dr. Coles coming with his wife and children.

Leona, however, had yet to bury the memories of harassment, although most of them dated from two years later. Her recollections were graphic and like her mother, Leona was and is a fighter:

> I knew of one woman who lived in back of us. She was fat and hateful. I was standing outside and she called me a "nigger." I called her "white" and she went and got the policeman who was watching our house. The policeman told her she better get along with people. Well, about six o'clock that evening that woman had everything out of her house and she moved.

A second example of harassment seemed humorous in retrospect:

There was one woman who works at the phone company. I have her picture at home in one of those scrapbooks. She's on top of a car; pregnant and screaming and hollering at us. I worked with her and I sat right next to her, and to this day she doesn't know it was me.

Leona considered her experience beneficial. It taught her tolerance, and how to get along with all kinds of people. From discussions, it appeared to me that she carried the school crisis more lightly than Ruby or even Tessie. This is reflected in her summary of the event: "Someone asked me once if I would let my kids do it. I guess I would. It was bad in a sense but it wasn't that bad. There are things that are worse. They were just 'hollerin.'"

Conclusion

All three of the families have been greatly affected by the event. When they enrolled their daughters in McDonogh 19 and Frantz, they had no way to anticipate the intensity of the hostility. As Dora Prevost said, "New Orleans had always been mixed; it seemed like the best place to integrate the schools." But for white New Orleanians, as it turned out, the schools were the last bastion of white separatism and superiority.

As integration spread, large numbers of whites enrolled their children in private schools or moved to the suburbs. The white community wanted to forget the school crisis so badly that not until twenty-three years later, in the spring of 1983, did the city even acknowledge the event. Then finally, the city publicly and officially recognized what Ruby Bridges, Tessie Prevost, Leona Tate, Gail Etiene, and their families had accomplished for integration in Louisiana.

Although the crisis shook the New Orleans schools, it was hardly a unique occurrence on a national scale. The importance of remembering it lies less in its demonstration of human vindictiveness, or even in its description of human suffering; rather, the biographies of these families depict an age of malaise for some and a time of struggle for others: an era of re-evaluation requiring a few to be courageous enough to confront injustice.

SECTION THREE

INTRODUCTORY NOTE

This section includes recent articles on race and education in South Carolina. Examples of racist textbooks, historical administrative racism, and the white hate groups are juxtaposed with accounts of racial diversity and changes that support and exemplify racial progress. Although the articles apply specifically to South Carolina, they mirror both the issues discussed in the previous sections and the racial issues that persist today throughout what Dick Gregory refers to as the "yet to be United States of America."

Chapter 10

South Carolina School History Textbooks' Portrayals of Race An Historical Analysis

Introduction

When Alabama governor Jim Folsom ordered the Confederate flag removed from atop the Alabama statehouse in May 1993, South Carolina became the only state that still flew the symbol of the Confederacy. Since that time a great deal of controversy has surrounded the flying of the flag. The issue has been debated in the state legislature, in newspaper articles, editorials, and letters to the editor, as well as on the streets of large cities and small towns throughout the state. Three white South Carolinians filed suit to remove the flag, and the national office of the NAACP announced that the organization is considering both legal action and an economic boycott of the state. Consideration of the history of the state that South Carolinians have learned through South Carolina history textbooks might help clarify the support of many South Carolinians for continuing to fly the flag. It might also help to explain the white racism that has characterized South Carolina and, to a degree, the rest of the nation. This chapter examines the portrayal of race, beginning with the textbooks South Carolina children read at the turn of the century and concluding with the two books currently in use.

Background

The South Carolina legislature passed laws in 1895 that made schooling compulsory for the state's children. The timing of this legislation corresponded to similar laws throughout the country. What made the timing of the South Carolina legislation noteworthy was that it corresponded with a flurry of laws now referred to as South Carolina's Black Codes of 1895. These laws severely limited the lives of African-Americans in the state though, of course, the legislation directly addressed only white children. One of the mandated subjects was South Carolina history, and at this time, in fact, most states were beginning to require history classes as part of the school curriculum. Frances Fitzgerald (1979) designated the 1890s "the Quattrocento of American-history-text writing" (p. 52). Fitzgerald's book *America Revised: History Schoolbooks in the Twentieth Century*, helps inform this chapter. But while Fitzgerald's work provides an extensive analysis of the content and changes of history textbooks throughout the twentieth century, the book's importance for our work is Fitzgerald's sensitivity to the significance of tone in the texts that she reviewed:

> In some general sense, this may be the truth of the matter: what sticks to the memory from those textbooks is not any particular series of facts but an atmosphere, an impression, a tone. And this impression may be all the more influential just because one cannot remember the facts and arguments that created it (p. 18).

The same point is made in I. A. Newby's book *Black Carolinians: A History of Blacks in South Carolina from 1895 to 1968* (1973). Newby's writing, though, specifically addresses South Carolina, race, and public-school histories.

> This was not a harmless exercise of the sort that makes public school history an agency for disseminating ordinary patriotic pieties. It was a serious business with serious results for both races. It inculcated in white Carolinians a set of historical "truths" that were always an obstacle to racial reform, while it poisoned, or sought to poison, the minds of blacks with assertions of their own inferiority and worthlessness (p. 7).

Newby's analysis powerfully illustrates the importance of tone in historical writing. He became even more critical, and we will return to that part of his work later, and his chapter, titled "White Supremacy," provides a short description and critique of South Carolina school history textbooks. The rest of this chapter will examine both the tone and the content of these textbooks as they address race.

The Textbooks

The legacy of South Carolina school history textbooks begins with William Gilmore Simms in the late nineteenth century. The Simms textbooks were updated and revised by Simms's granddaughter, Mary C. Simms Oliphant, through the 1960s. Other early-twentieth-century books included John J. Dargan's *School History of South Carolina*, John Langdon Weber's *Fifty Lessons in the History of South Carolina*, John Chapman's *School History of South Carolina*, and Henry Alexander White's *The Making of South Carolina*. Presently there are two texts that are approved by the State Department of Education; Lewis P. Jones's *South Carolina: One of the Fifty States* and Archie Vernon Huff Jr.'s *The History of South Carolina in the Building of the Nation* (Dargan, 1906; Weber, 1891; Chapman, 1895; White, 1906; Simms, 1917, 1922; Oliphant, 1922, 1940, 1958, 1970; Jones, 1985; Huff, 1991).

Topics

Discussion of race is very minimal in all of these texts for the years preceding 1800. There are discussions of Slavery as it existed before the Civil War and limited discussion of Race Relations and Free Blacks. Reconstruction is dealt with in greater detail as is the Jim Crow period in the books that were printed after World War I. Discussion of the Civil Rights Movement and School Integration are subject material for the current texts.

The Turn-of-the Century Texts

South Carolina used four history textbooks early in the twentieth century, the presentation of each corresponds to the general description Fitzgerald provided for the American history textbooks of the time (pp. 51–52). One finds attempts at personal portraits, but the prevalent tone is dry and the books offer orderly, sometimes even numbered, narratives of histori-

cal events. The exception is that each becomes positively ver-
bose when discussing negative aspects of the African-American slaves and of radical reconstruction.

The Turn-of-the Century Texts — Slavery

Thus far we have said little of the tone(s) of these discussions.
Accordingly, these early texts receive strong criticism in *Black
Carolinians*, where Newby quoted John Dargan's *School History
of South Carolina*: "The importation of African slaves to America
is the most grievous misfortune that ever befell the white race
in any part of the world" (pp. 10–11). Newby had been discussing the descriptions by Dargan and his colleagues of the "good
master" and "lucky slave" and he cited Dargan to illustrate a
point of view and tone that both failed to address the harsh
realities of slavery for African-Americans, and tended to blame
the slaves for troubling white South Carolinians. Dargan discusses slavery in three chapters: "Slavery," "Negro Insurrec-
tions," and "Causes of Secession." The "Slavery" chapter is only
seven pages of which five discuss economics, morality, the
South as the moral equivalent of the North, and the greatest
abolitionists who, of course, were South Carolinians. Unlike
the more recent texts, Dargan neglected to discuss the Grimke
sisters or the Quaker ministers who left the state because of
the abolitionists activities. One can't help but think "he pro-
tests too much."

In Dargan's text, when slaves are finally introduced, albeit
briefly, we find a discussion of how much they loved their
masters. Thus, the Stono Rebellion and Denmark Vesey each
receive a paragraph, each introduced as extreme exceptions
to the rule. Two of the page headings capture Dargan's point:
"Loyalty of the Slaves" and "Slaves Were Content." As an after-
thought, he wrote that if slaves had revolted during the Civil
War, the Union army would have stood by their white brothers
against the Blacks. Allowing for the fact that Dargan wrote at
the turn-of-the century, his description of what a Black insur-
rection would have been like confirms Newby's analysis of white
racist histories:

> had outrage and slaughter been attempted by the negro slaves upon
> the white women and children of the South, Northern soldiers by the

thousands would have joined the soldiers of the South to protect the white race . . . The negro acted wisely, as well as in accordance with his kindly nature (p. 129).

One finds no discussion of slavery hardships or of any white racist attrocities by South Carolinians in Dargan's text. His tone implies good white slaveowners and Blacks who were fortunate to have been slaves in South Carolina:

As to the effect on the slave, it must be admitted that slavery did for the negro what nothing else could have done—it brought him here and partially civilized him. Whoever else may abhor the institution, the negro everywhere should turn to it with gratitude (p. 126).

The other texts students read at the turn-of-the century addressed slavery even less than Dargan's book. Weber mentioned Denmark Vesey and John Brown as did Chapman while White's book mentioned slavery only in the context of the need for Africans to grow rice:

It was found that white men lost their health if they tried to work in the swamp lands. Negroes from Africa, however, were able to work in the rice fields without any injury to themselves. For this reason large numbers of Negroes were brought from Africa to South Carolina. Without their help the rice could not have been cultivated (p. 22).

None of these books discussed slavery in any detail.

John Chapman's analysis of the Emancipation Proclamation displays a representative tone and is also a good link to the early-twentieth-century texts writing on Reconstruction:

Whether Mr. Lincoln so meant it or not, cannot now be said, but this Emancipation Proclamation can hardly be read with any other understanding than that it was a direct call upon the slaves to assert and maintain their freedom, by any means in their power, even by the indiscriminate slaughter of helpless women and children, if they felt it necessary (p. 192).

The Turn-of-the Century Texts—Reconstruction

The tone of the textbooks discussed became even harsher when describing Reconstruction. Dargan titled the chapter "The Dark Days" while Weber had a section titled "The Reign of Plunderers." Dargan was extremely critical:

> So there came early into this field, to ply their nefarious arts; the "carpet-bagger"—the soulless oppressor from the North—and the "scalawag"—the soulless plunderer from the South—and for nearly ten years in South Carolina 'they robbed while they pretended to rule; they plundered while they professed to protect,' until the State became so reduced in material strength and so dispirited under the heavy weight of such conditions that it was known as the "Prostrate State" (pp. 151–153).

The above quotation begins on page 151 and ends on 153. On 152 is a photograph titled, "The Black (Radical) Legislature." Dargan described the legislators:

> It was quite bad enough to have ignorant negroes in the Legislature as a law-making power, as judges in our highest and our lowest courts, presiding over our Senatorial bodies and serving as Speakers of the House of Representatives, and as Members of Congress (p. 153).

Midway through the chapter Wade Hampton rides in as the rational white hero—much the way Newby describes white South Carolinians treatment of heroes and very similar to Dargan's own portrayal of South Carolina abolitionists. Dargan described it as the "overthrow of that 'blackest abomination'" (p. 155). He concluded his section on Reconstruction with a discussion of the Ku Klux Klan that began with Dargan stating the necessity of historical honesty:

> It is not proper, nor will a faithful historian try, to evade matters of error on the part of the people of whom he writes; and if we conceived that there were great errors and outrages committed in the Kuklux Klan movement, we should feel none the less under obligations to give it a place in this history, frankly telling of the injury done by its existence (p. 159).

Dargan's presentation of the Klan continued with the views of two South Carolina Klan leaders; the first, General N. B. Forrest, who Dargan wrote "is universally regarded as one of the loftiest and most chivalrous characters in American history" (p. 155). The second was General John B. Gordon, who according to Dargan "was one of the most beloved citizens in the Union" (p. 155). For both generals the Ku Klux Klan was a defensive and necessary organization that was forced into existence to "protect the white people 'against dangers from the blacks, incited to hostility and violence by alien whites of low character'" (pp. 160-161). We can only assume that Dargan believed that there was no "injury done by its existence." What we can't understand, knowing his point of view, is why he began his discussion of the Klan with an historical caveat?

Weber's section headings (like "The Reign of Plunderers" noted above and followed by "The Prince of the Thieves" on the two governors of the Union-appointed South Carolina government) are rather spicy but the numbered paragraphs in each section are somewhat boring and it is very difficult to imagine them keeping the attention of schoolchildren. As to content, Weber, like Dargan, portrayed duped former slaves helping the carpetbaggers and scalawags hurt the noble and moral lives of white South Carolinians. White provided a similar portrait but his writing was more powerful. The following is from his discussion of Black soldiers: "The rule of these armed negroes was a grievous burden. They were unjust and cruel and shot down many quiet white citizens" (p. 290). He concluded, of course, just like Dargan and Weber, with Wade Hampton again coming in and saving the state. Before Hampton, though, there was a final discussion of Reconstruction:

> More than half of the members of the legislature were negroes, and most of these could neither read nor write. They spent nearly all of their time in the legislature stealing the money of the people. Thousands and thousands of dollars were taken by these black thieves. Neither the property nor the lives of white people were safe anywhere in the state (p. 293).

Finally, Chapman began with a subsection on northern reactions to the Black Codes of 1865. As he discussed the federal government entering South Carolina he wondered in print whether the Black Codes were a pretext or the reason for intrusion. Like the other texts, discussion of race ends with the coming to power of Wade Hampton.

The Turn-of-the Century Texts—Conclusion

Although race was a primary issue in South Carolina between Reconstruction and the turn of the century, the texts that children read before World War I saw race after Reconstruction as a non-issue. One should remember that all four of the authors were white southerners and with the exception of

Chapman all lived and taught in South Carolina. Although Jim
Crow was a taboo subject, their portraits of ignorant but happy
slaves reinforced a white supremist world view. Southern writers were not alone, however, as it took until the 1970s for the
treatment of slavery and Reconstruction to change in American history textbooks throughout the country. Frances
Fitzgerald described American history textbook writing on the
subject as similar to the four books just discussed:

> According to these books, Radical Reconstruction was an unmitigated
> disaster. The Reconstruction governments were imposed on the South
> with federal bayonets and were run by a lot of unscrupulous "carpet-
> baggers" and "scalawags." Instead of reconstructing the region, they
> pillaged it. The legislatures—filled with ignorant Negroes who obeyed
> the dictates of the carpetbaggers and scalawags—engaged in an "orgy
> of spending. . . ." The tremendous corruption of these governments,
> combined with the anarchy caused by bands of Negroes roaming the
> countryside, finally forced the Southerners to take action (p. 86).

Newby's analysis of South Carolina history provides a more
localized means to appraise the early twentieth century. This,
of course, was a time period of numerous lynchings, of Black
Codes designed to suppress Black South Carolinians, and of a
state legislature that in 1913 petitioned the United States Congress to repeal the Fifteenth Amendment with the following
words:

> In return for the right to vote, resolved the Assemblymen, blacks have
> given America nothing but "anxiety, strife, bloodshed, and the hook-
> worm" (p. 44).

In concluding this section on the Turn of the Century textbooks, we again examine Newby's *Black Carolinians* for insights
into the four dominant texts. Newby explained why white
supremists resisted any moderation of their views. He concluded with words that might as well apply to Dargan, Weber,
White and Chapman:

> The price of white supremacy, like the price of liberty, was eternal
> vigilance. Blacks had to be taught to resign themselves to white
> supremacy, and the lesson, so easily forgotten, had to be regularly
> repeated (p. 45).

The Simms–Oliphant Texts

William Gilmore Simms first published a South Carolina history textbook for the state's schoolchildren in 1840. Simms died in 1912 and his granddaughter, Mary C. Simms Oliphant, continued the tradition of her grandfather's book by first revising and editing the text in 1917. At least one revision appeared in each decade of the twentieth century, and the final edition of the book was published in 1970. Some changes occurred each decade, but the tone of the textbook's treatment of race remained consistent. As we examine the changes, note the general "cheerleading" tone of the Simms–Oliphant texts. It should come as no surprise that Ms. Oliphant also wrote South Carolina tourism books.

The Simms–Oliphant Texts—Slavery

The 1917 and 1922 texts are very similar and lack the intensity of the earlier texts when they champion the cause of good South Carolina slaveholders. One finds important textual difference in the two editions, however. The first edition includes a quote from philosopher John Locke that justifies slavery as an institution: "'Every freeman of Carolina,' he wrote, 'shall have absolute power and authority over his negro slaves'" (p. 75). But the 1922 text admits the evils of slavery as an institution. The former edition seems drier and issues statements with little description. Both editions describe slaves as heathens and property, and both present and discuss a law that taxed "negroes, liquors, and other goods and merchandise" (1922, p. 57). The 1917 text briefly mentioned the Stono Rebellion and white fear, but this disappeared from the 1922 edition. The second text's description of slave life is juxtaposed across the page from an elaborate explanation of the riches and glamour of white plantation life (pp. 146-147). Portraits of slavery in both editions described slave housing and work and included the following passage on how slaves were treated:

> As we shall hear much a little later on about the evils of slavery, it should be said now that the slave owners in South Carolina, as a rule, treated their negroes with the greatest kindness, fed them well and clothed them comfortably. A negro slave cost money and a slave owner

would no more have thought of mistreating a slave and making him unfit to work than he would have thought of abusing a fine horse (1922, p. 146).

Further discussions of slavery acknowledged that slavery was wrong but, in the tradition of the early-twentieth-century texts, asserted that the slave benefited and that northern influences forced southerners and white South Carolinians in particular into defending the institution. After a discussion of the economic need to continue slavery in the state, the Simms texts broached morality and concluded with a racist twist:

It must be understood that it was the custom of the day to hold slaves. . . . There is no doubt that holding human beings in slavery was a great wrong even though it civilized the savage negroes who were brought over from Africa (1922, p. 161).

Simms and Oliphant placed a measure of blame on the Underground Railroad and abolitionist pamphleteers for the hardening of white South Carolinians' views on slavery. Mention is made but no detail provided on *Uncle Tom's Cabin* or John Brown in either edition. Nat Turner receives brief treatment with the emphasis on the resentment of white South Carolinians to northern interference:

The attitude of this section towards slavery began to change. Southerners would no longer admit the evil of holding slaves. They emphasized the fact that slavery had taken savages into a civilized, Christian land. They brought out the fact that before these negroes came to the South they had never even heard of Christ. Their masters had taught them how to till the soil and how to live a useful life (1922, p. 179).

Before moving to the Simms–Oliphant histories of the 1930s and 1940s, one should note that although the topics and views of the 1917 and 1922 books are similar, a difference in tone exists. The former book appears generally content to present information while the latter is far more descriptive.

The 1932 and 1940 editions of the Simms–Oliphant texts used essentially the same discussions as the earlier texts to address slavery. The 1940 book, however, took a slightly different tone when discussing the Underground Railroad and abolitionism: They are less forcefully accused of hardening white South Carolinians' support of slavery. In fact, a new section, "South Carolina's Mistake," lists two mistaken "cherished beliefs":

> First, they felt that slave labor was necessary to the South because farming was the chief interest of this section; second, South Carolinians honestly believed that there were so many slaves that their freedom would mean that the South would belong to the black race (1940, p. 227).

The 1958 and 1970 texts show more sophistication and were no longer published by the State Company in Columbia but rather by Laidlaw Brothers in River Forest, Illinois. The tone of these two texts lowers the boosterism, and the 1970 text is more subdued than the 1958 edition when discussing external reasons for the hardening of white South Carolinian's views on slavery. In fact, where the 1917 and 1922 editions emphasized the position that the abolitionists hardened local support of slavery, one finds hardly a hint of that viewpoint in the later texts. The 1958 text bemoaned the need for slaves to work in the rice fields and the 1970 book repeated its predecessors with the story of whites not being able to work in the field. It adds that the Africans became proficient at this task. Both texts discuss the duties and the treatment of the slaves and the 1970 text includes this familiar argument from previous editions:

> Most masters treated their slaves kindly. In fact, it did not make sense to treat them any other way. A slave was a costly investment, and it was to the master's interest to keep him contented and well (1970, p. 116).

The 1970 discussion continued about food and health care but at last Ms. Oliphant abandoned the 1922 comparison of a healthy slave to a valuable horse. Exceptions to beneficent treatment are used to introduce the Stono Rebellion, its first treatment in these texts since the 1917 edition. The 1958 and 1970 editions are also the first to introduce Denmark Vesey; the passages speak of white fear but the topic is handled rationally and without any portrayal of terror. The abolitionists, *Uncle Tom's Cabin*, and John Brown receive attention but the Underground Railroad and fugitive slaves disappear. The former topics represent contributors to white South Carolinians' bitterness and resentment though one finds none of the intensity of previous editions. The absence of the Underground Railroad is significant because it had earlier served as a major cause for hardening white South Carolinians' views of slavery. The 1970 text also included the story of Robert Small with a picture of his boat. Although neither book is pro-Abolitionist or anti-white South Carolina, they do provide a more impartial portrayal of slavery than the editions we discussed earlier.

The Simms–Oliphant Texts—Reconstruction

The Reconstruction chapter in both the 1917 and the 1922 edition is titled "South Carolina Under Radical Government." Both begin with South Carolina's "benevolent" attempt to give emancipated slaves some rights, but also with the need for control:

> The State was willing to give the negro equal protection under the law, but was decidedly unwilling to allow him to vote and sit on juries. The negroes were in such large majority that giving the vote to them was not to be considered. The State had a tremendous problem to face in the sudden freeing of thousands of irresponsible, uneducated, unmoral, and, in many cases brutish Africans. The people of South Carolina felt that they were a danger and that harsh laws were necessary to hold them in bounds (1922, pp. 212–213).

Like the turn-of-the-century texts, the tone is quite clear in both editions although the second edition is more overstated. The carpetbaggers and scalawags are portrayed as thieves and plunderers and the freed slaves are viewed as their dupes. The following chapter in both editions is titled "Overthrow of Radical Government." Both editions begin with a discussion of the need for the Ku Klux Klan and of the federal government's wronging of the KKK when they were punished for their attacks on Blacks:

> Secret organizations of white men were formed in nearly all the conquered states of the South. The men in these organizations were determined to hold the freed slaves in check and to fight the evil-doing radicals. These secret organizations were called the Ku-Klux Klan. . . . The Ku-Klux Klan secretly decided to oppose the radicals as well as to protect the women and children of the State. The Ku-Klux Klan met only at night. They were always mounted on horses and wore caps and masks to conceal their faces and long white coats which covered them and fell down over their horses. The sight of these ghostly

riders galloping by in the night was a very terrifying one to the super-
stitious negro. A visit from the Ku-Klux was sufficient in most cases
to turn him away from his evil doing (1922, p. 220).

There is discussion of Black abominations and violence and
the criminal acts of Franklin Moses. Like the turn-of-the-century texts, however, all is made good with the coming to power
of Wade Hampton. A picture of a statue of Hampton on his
horse appears on page 225 of the 1922 edition. In both editions there are brief sections on the Constitution of 1895 and
although there is not enough material for a discussion of Jim
Crow, the paragraph on the Constitution is an appropriate
way to conclude the discussion of this edition:

> This was necessary so as to give white people protection against an
> overwhelming and illiterate majority of negroes in the State (1922,
> p. 241).

The 1932 edition changed very little. There was a new paragraph on how much the emancipated slaves still loved their
masters, but the sections on the carpetbaggers and scalawags
and the Reconstruction (Radical) government are unchanged.
The passage on the Ku Klux Klan that is cited above added an
additional line. "Many of the best men in South Carolina belonged to the Ku Klux Klan" (p. 245). This is similar to Dargan's
book, but interestingly it was not stated or implied in the prior
edition. Hampton is again the savior; however, the view of the
statue, which appears on page 250, is this time from afar with
Trinity Cathedral in the background. The 1895 Constitution
is mentioned but without the racist justification and there is
one topic mentioned, sharecropping, that was not mentioned
in previous editions. The tone of the descriptions of the time
preceding Wade Hampton is as harsh as the previous two editions, only this time we are spared the racist explanation of
the need for the 1895 Black Codes.

The 1940 edition is almost exactly the same as the 1932
book when addressing Reconstruction. This edition, though,
offers a denigrating description of Blacks to rationalize the
need for the 1895 Black Codes:

> There were more Negroes than whites in the State. The Negroes were
> uneducated. They had no knowledge of government. They did not
> know how to make a living without the supervision of the white man.

They were so accustomed to being taken care of that they had no idea how to behave under freedom. They stole cattle and chickens and hogs, burned barns and stables. They were not willing to work. They were like children playing hookey the moment the teacher's back was turned. There were so many more Negroes than whites that they would have been in control if they had been allowed to vote. They had nearly ruined the State during the years they had voted. The whites were determined that this should not happen again. Regulations were made which prevented the Negroes from voting, and to this day South Carolina has a white man's government (p. 265).

Black illiteracy is again discussed later in the book. What is interesting is that Ms. Oliphant felt the need to add this passage after just mentioning the 1895 Constitution in the prior edition.

The Reconstruction chapter in both the 1958 and the 1970 Simms–Oliphant text titled "The Ordeal of Reconstruction." Each begins by restating good relations between white South Carolinians and emancipated slaves: "Most of the slaves had proved their affection for and loyalty to their masters" (1958, p. 275). Both editions discuss giving Blacks the vote as a problem that white South Carolinians had to deal with, and both texts viewed the initial post–Civil War Black Codes as a mistake:

As it turned out, this was not a wise decision. Even more unwise were the laws passed by the state legislature to regulate the conduct of the former slaves (1958, p. 277).

The carpetbaggers and scalawags are again discussed and although the criticism is extremely understated in relationship to the previous editions, both the 1958 and the 1970 text reprints a grotesque Thomas Nast cartoon of a carpetbagger with the caption "A cartoon by Thomas Nast indicates the low esteem in which carpetbaggers were held" (1958, p. 278). In contrast, the 1970 edition adds the following line to its introduction of the carpetbaggers. "Some were no doubt well intentioned" (p. 286).

Both texts are critical of the Radical legislature, albeit more subtly than previous texts, and critical of the ignorance of the freed Blacks. The Ku Klux Klan is again introduced and although the message of the KKK as a white protector is consistent with the previous editions, the portrayal is half as long and written as something that has to be stated but does not have to be elaborated upon. Finally, as in the other editions discussion ends with Hampton coming in and working for the good of South Carolina. The 1970s text has an additional section, "Progress of the Negro," which introduces political leaders, professionals, and churchmen with short biographies. Both texts mention Tillman and the 1895 Constitution and both texts address schooling in the mid-twentieth century. This last discussion includes three topics: 1. The dual school system which both editions claimed was a system of equal schools in the cities but not in rural South Carolina. 2. Governor Byrnes's attempt to solidify "separate but equal" by building new Black schools. 3. And finally, the *Brown* decision and this final quote on school integration.

> After long, drawn-out desegregation suits in the courts, South Carolina now has an integrated school system for pupils of all races (1958, p. 375).

The Simms–Oliphant Texts—Conclusion

Since these textbooks covered a period of nearly 80 years one hesitates to make broad generalizations. But a case could be made that the textbooks changed much the same way American history textbooks have changed and continue to change. We will return to this discussion in the conclusion. It might be important, though, to add the fact that the Simms–Oliphant textbooks were written for South Carolina children by a nineteenth-century white South Carolinian and his twentieth-century granddaughter, both of whom loved the state and its heritage and tradition. The connections between the heritage William Gilmore Simms and Mary C. Simms Oliphant venerated and white racism in South Carolina will also be evaluated in the conclusion.

The Current Texts

The South Carolina State Department of Education currently approves two texts: *South Carolina: One of the Fifty States* (1985) by Lewis P. Jones, and Archie Vernon Huff Jr.'s *The History of South Carolina in the Building of the Nation* (1991). Both address

slavery and Reconstruction. The current texts devote time to
Jim Crow and both books deal with twentieth-century issues
and the civil rights movement in South Carolina. The style
and the spirit of these texts are, however, quite different. Jones,
a history professor at Wofford College, and his editors at
Sandlapper Publishing have produced a "slick Madison Avenue
textbook" in the new tradition that Frances Fitzgerald describes
in *America Revised*. Jones's book falls short of replicating *Ar-
chitectural Digest* or *Vogue*, but its graphics and illustrations are
highly sophisticated, more sophisticated certainly than those
in the Huff book, its contemporary. While Fitzgerald's conclusion would be an exaggeration when comparing the Jones
and Huff texts, it is accurate enough to convey the right idea:

> Whereas in the nineteen-fifties the texts were childish in the sense
> that they were naive and clumsy, they are now childish in the sense
> that they are polymorphous-perverse. American history is not dull
> any longer; it is a sensuous experience (p. 16).

Marketing and modernity aside, the Jones text, more than
Huff's, continues the tradition of racism in South Carolina
history textbooks. Style becomes ironic in this situation because the Huff book is in the tradition of 1950s textbooks sty-
listically and is, in fact, dedicated to Mary C. Simms Oliphant.
Although the book is by no means a sensitive multicultural
textbook, it provides a more thoughtful and equitable analysis
of race in South Carolina.

The Current Texts—Slavery

Huff's treatment of slavery begins with a description of the
slave trade and offers this interesting characterization of African diversity:

> Few of the slaves brought directly from Africa knew English. They
> belonged to many tribal groups. For example, some were Ebos, some
> Angolans, and others Gambians. They spoke many African dialects;
> some spoke Arabic. Many worshiped the spirits of their ancestors in
> the African tradition (p. 70).

This passage, and Huff's book in general, offers no great insights into race in South Carolina. Passages like this do, how-

ever, open possibilities for teachers to infuse African and African-American culture and history into South Carolina history.

Jones treatment of slavery begins with the early nineteenth century. He introduces abolitionist voices including the Grimke sisters and contributes short biographies of two pro-slavery preachers, James Thornwell and Ben Palmer (p. 377). Jones uses bold outlined and shaded boxes throughout the text for special effect and many of these are subtly or not so subtly racist. In his early discussion of slavery the first box is labeled "SLAVERY: NOT ALWAYS A PROFIT." We will return to these boxes shortly and it will become apparent that the tone of the antislavery boxes and the boxes about white South Carolinians differ markedly.

Both texts introduce the Nullification Crisis and Jones offers an interesting analysis of South Carolina's radical white secessionists:

> The ghost of Denmark Vesey still haunted these alarmed men. As individuals, many South Carolina leaders were attractive, honorable, and certainly sincere. In light of their past and the society of which they were a part, their viewpoint and their unwillingness to change it are understandable. Nevertheless, in their fears and inflexible determination to maintain their society, they were dangerous men—dangerous to others and dangerous to that same society (p. 402).

This is one of only a few passages in the entire Jones book that are mildly critical of white South Carolinians. Huff's discussion of the same topic is less wordy, and the only memorable statement is Charles Pinckney's remark that slavery would lead to civil war.

Both Jones and Huff also address slave rebellions and white South Carolinians' fear of Blacks. Both cover the Stono Rebellion in Charleston, John Brown, and Denmark Vesey, but the books prompt different responses. Jones stresses the justification of white fear, and in his discussion of the slave rebellions, he begins to sound the note of a blameless white South Carolinia. This attitude gives his book a racist undertone and it continues as Jones discusses Reconstruction and the beginnings of Jim Crow. Consider this brief portrait of John Brown:

> In 1859, a fanatic drove the South into a frenzy. John Brown, an unbalanced abolitionist, with a tiny "army" launched a rebellion at

Harper's Ferry, Virginia, and called for slaves to rise and join the movement. John Brown's raid was quickly nipped in the bud and was not supported by the North. But it convinced Southerners of their worst fears concerning slave rebellions and abolitionists (p. 454).

Jones continues by comparing southerners' view of Brown with northerners' view of Simon Legree, thus, again implying that there was no absolute right or wrong when it came to slavery, just differing points of view. Huff discusses white fear but he accords it less justification than Jones. A painting of Denmark Vesey appears on page 206 and the Grimke sisters are pictured on the next page. Instead of emphasizing white fear, Huff discusses the 1840 laws enacted specifically to suppress Blacks. Even when he compares northern and southern views of John Brown one finds a tolerant tone. "To the Southerners he was a symbol of the desire of the North to end slavery. To Northern abolitionists Brown was a saint and martyr" (p. 251).

Both books briefly describe the lives of South Carolina slaves. Huff uses chapter-ending sections labeled "Eyewitness to History" to present short biographical sketches. One of these sections reproduces a letter written in 1875 by an emancipated slave named Sancho Cooper. The subtitle is "Sancho Cooper Becomes a Slave" and the letter discusses life as a slave and the importance of religion. Huff devotes two other pages to describing the life of the slave.

Jones's book contains more description with a four-page section depicting slave life on the plantation. Although he does not write that slave life was difficult for Blacks, he includes this paragraph on the burdensome life of the overseer:

> Normally a crude and uncultured person, the overseer was the key individual in disciplining and managing plantation slaves. Seeking to please the owner and yet not to oppress the slaves, he couldn't win. If he drove the slaves too hard, they would rebel. He could not supervise every detail of every slaves' life and be everywhere at once. He rarely had time away from his task, and hence it is not surprising that on many plantations there were frequent turnovers of overseers (p. 426).

Jones certainly resists glorifying the overseer but his presentation of the trials and tribulations of the position parallels his analysis of the difficult life innocent white South Carolinians faced preceding, during, and after the Civil War.

Both Jones and Huff discuss white South Carolina leaders like Calhoun and their positions on race, and they both discuss abolitionism as well. Huff bemoans the lack of leadership in the country, meaning that Clay, Webster, and Calhoun were gone and they were replaced by "southern fire-eaters" and "northern abolitionists" (p. 248). In the chapter introducing "Life in the Antebellum Years," Huff writes, "Planters dominated the state, but small farmers, poor whites, and African Americans made major contributions to society" (p. 213). He introduces Massachusetts free-Black abolitionist David Walker, William Lloyd Garrison, and the Grimke sisters. Jones introduces abolitionism as a force that galvanized and fortified the white South Carolinian slavery advocates:

> The more the Abolitionists up North screamed, the more the Southerners fell back on rationalizing or excusing. Extremism always gives birth to extremism (p. 428).

We see here another instance of Jones declining to place responsibility with white South Carolinians. The discussion of abolitionism provides the beginning of the FAN THE FLAME bold faced and shaded boxes described earlier. The effect is strongly racist because what stands out as bad is either Black or northern, always under the title of FAN THE FLAMES. The remaining boxes, the ones that do not Fan the Flames, record the sensitivity of South Carolina whites. This first box is labeled "The Grimke Sisters Fan the Flames: 1839." The text inside the box introduces the Grimke's, *Slavery as It Is: The Testimony of a Thousand Witnesses*. Jones writes that the sisters had scanned newspaper articles in the South for articles on the cruelties of slavery. He calls it an unfair tactic because it made the South testify against itself (p. 454).

Two pages after the Grimke sisters' box, another appears labeled "Opinion-Makers Fan the Flames." Jones explains that famous writers "added their voices and influence to the abolitionist movement" (p. 456). Inside of the box is the poem "The Slave Ships" by John Greenleaf Whittier. On the following page Calhoun's speech "Africanization of the South" is quoted in reference to the need to stop the antislavery movement (p. 457). Jones then uses Harriet Beecher Stowe's *Uncle Tom's Cabin* as an illustration of a book that hardened the southerners slavery views. This troubling attitude prompts the following quote:

"More and more the South then sought to defend slavery as a good system blessed and desired by God" (p. 458). For Jones, the defense of slavery is a natural response to northern extremism, a position that allows him, and the eighth-grade students who read his texts, to avoid the responsibility for analyzing history objectively.

Huff spends little time on slavery during the Civil War, with only some discussion of Black troops and an introduction to Robert Small. But Jones produces another FAN THE FLAMES box: "Blacks Fan the Flames." He includes short passages condemning slavery but the loud, prominent title overwhelms the content and sets up antislavery people as the troublemakers (p. 460). One more FAN THE FLAMES box is titled "Northerners Fan the Flames." Compare it with a box titled "A Southern Conscience." The content of the latter box is inconsequential because the contrast between the titles is so extreme. Still, in the latter box Jones uses Mary Chesnut's *Diary from Dixie* as a source and presents a thoughtful discussion of white missionaries positive view of the emancipated slaves before moving to a discussion of Reconstruction.

Huff's portrait of race and slavery, to repeat, is less than notably insightful or thoughtful. Neither does it condemn African-Americans or elevate white South Carolinians, as the turn-of-the-century texts did. Jones, too, declines to present a glowing portrait of white South Carolinians during slavery. But he spends little space describing slavery or individual African-Americans at all. Moreover, one finds a major flaw in his work on slavery: That flaw, which continues in his discussion of Reconstruction, is that he neglects to condemn the practice. In fact, he provides reasons for the continuing support white South Carolinians expressed for slavery.

The Current Texts—Reconstruction

Huff's and Jones's tones differ in their chapters on Reconstruction—the Reconstruction period the turn-of-the-century texts refer to as "Black Reconstruction." Huff begins with a very brief discussion of Black inclusion and reprints the disparaging Thomas Nast cartoon of a carpetbagger as well as a painting of the Ku Klux Klan attacking three African-Americans. Next to Nast's cartoon is the question: "What was Nast's view of carpetbaggers?" (p. 281) The caption to the Klan picture reads: "The Ku Klux Klan began as a social club and soon became an organization spreading terror among Black freedmen" (p. 281). Huff's explanations are clear as his chapter on Reconstruction. Huff discusses the same themes that are discussed in most American history textbooks; carpetbaggers, scalawags, emancipated slaves, education, the Black church, and moderate and extreme white reactions to Reconstruction. Like the historians that preceded him, Huff documents Wade Hampton coming to power and he labels 1877 to 1890 as the conservative years:

> In South Carolina white conservatives were in power from 1877 to 1890. At first, they followed Hampton's moderate racism, but later they sought ways to keep blacks out of politics. The Conservatives kept the memory of the "Lost Cause" alive while they welcomed the industrial age they called the New South (p. 295).

Huff is honest in his appraisal of Wade Hampton and although he doesn't examine any of the Blacks who participated in Reconstruction in any depth, he does quote Robert Small's speech at the Constitutional Convention of 1895:

> My race needs no special defense, for the past history of them in this country proves them to be the equal of people anywhere. All they need is an equal chance in the battle of life (p. 336).

Although Robert Small is mentioned in Jones's book, there is no mention of the speech cited above. Jones's Reconstruction chapter continues with the same tone that was evident in the section on slavery, the continuing conflict between North and South. Again, it was northern attitudes that lead to southern resentment. "The victors were determined not so much to reconstruct the South as they were determined to stifle (suppress) antebellum attitudes and policies in the South" (p. 504). He creates a negative picture of the emancipated slaves and then blames Reconstruction for the continuance of white racism at the present time. Does this connect to the FAN THE FLAMES boxes? Is the white racism that exists in South Carolina in the late twentieth century the result of northern and Black influences during Reconstruction? As preposterous as it appears, that is what Jones alludes to. Might descriptions of the emancipated slaves, like those that Jones supplies in his text, be a more probable cause for South Carolina racism at the present time? Consider his description:

> Unprepared for their new status, lacking education needed to improve their role in society, frustrated by being downtrodden in a region now itself crushed and poverty-ridden, blacks faced a bleak future despite their new freedom in their "Day of Jubilee" (p. 505).

This isn't presented to deny that there isn't some truth in Jones's description. Personally, I would have preferred the Robert Small speech that Huff quotes because it is a more honest example of possibilities for Blacks when given a chance. The problem with Jones's analysis is that it presents a totally negative view of the emancipated slave and implies blame on northern whites and Black people themselves rather than providing an honest presentation of the horrors of slavery or the later horrors of Jim Crow.

Jones continues with an informative discussion on the carpetbaggers and provides thoughtful portraits of two Blacks, Richard Cain and Martin Delaney. He quotes a Black politician on the responsibility of Blacks in power not to become scoundrels. Interestingly, he perceives no need for the same warning for white politicians. Again, Jones makes interesting choices of what is important for his readers. He covers the general topics that we listed above and concludes the chapter with what would be insightful historiography if taken at face value; unfortunately it is a direct contradiction to both his account of slavery and of Reconstruction. It is necessary to quote at length:

> For half a century, most accounts of the period were biased and often inaccurate. Many were written to stir fears and to strengthen white determination to prevent any change in the society which they had redeemed by ending the political reconstruction. . . . The manner in which later generations learned their history, the views and the ideas that people had about 1865-1877, affected their thinking, their attitudes, their prejudices, their actions. People's understanding of Reconstruction thus was more important than was Reconstruction itself, because it has had so much influence on the years since 1877. Studying history, you see, puts real responsibility on the reader or the student. Much of the grief of South Carolina in the last hundred

years has come from its own misreading of its history. For a state with
so much decency, it should have been spared that (pp. 525–527).

Jones's quotation which concludes his writing on Reconstruction left me speechless upon first reading. All that I could think of was whether or not he even realized that much of his description of both slavery and Reconstruction were prime examples of FANNING THE FLAME.

The Current Texts—Jim Crow

Both textbooks begin this section with chapters on Tillmanism. Huff's is called, "Tillman and the Rise of Farmers" while Jones's chapter has the interesting title "Tillmanism: A Political Departure." Whether or not Jones's title is historically accurate is open to debate, but the chapter does present a thoughtful and critical description of the oppression of African-Americans. The 1895 Black Codes are presented, as is a discussion on the increase of lynchings. Jones presents statistics on Black illiteracy and poverty and describes Black life in a section titled "Less Happy Side of Life: Bleakness for Blacks." This is followed by a section on Black leadership that presents South Carolinians in the tradition of Booker T. Washington. The text discusses Black emigration to the North and Jones concludes the chapter in two ways. First he uses a box to explain why he had to present so much on race; oddly, he actually gave race little exposure. He finishes with a conversation on racism and stereotyping. As in all preceding discussions, Jones cannot put the blame squarely on the shoulders of white South Carolinians. In this case he has to equivocate:

> Too long in South Carolina, both whites and blacks have lacked the patience for that kind of approach. And all have been the worse for it. As a wise person put it once, the only way to keep another person down in a ditch is to get down in the ditch with that person (p. 597).

Huff's chapter discusses the 1895 all-white primary, *Plessy* v *Ferguson*, and chooses Booker T. Washington as the consummate role model. It is important to stress, however, that throughout the book Huff's tone places much of the blame for slavery and racism on white South Carolinians. On Tillman's inaugural speech, he says:

> . . . he urged a law against lynching, that is, mob violence against blacks. But he also made very clear his views on race. Jefferson was wrong when he said all men were created equal. Blacks were not equal. "The whites have absolute control of the State Government," Tillman said, "and we intend . . . to retain it" (p. 333).

Although the contrast between the two books is not as great when discussing Jim Crow, there are examples of the same differences in tone as noted above: Huff is harder on white South Carolinians and offers a more compassionate picture of Blacks in the state, while Jones finds it impossible to declare white South Carolinians responsible for racism.

The Current Texts—The Civil Rights Movement

There is very little mention of race in either text's review of the twentieth century up until the civil rights movement. Some Black leaders like Benjamin Mays and Mary Mcleod Bethune are introduced, but the treatment is at best cursory. Both texts introduce the *Brown* decision and white resistance and they both discuss civil rights sit-ins and Judge Waties Warings decision against the state's white primary. Both Jones and Huff present Governor Byrnes's attempt to build new Black schools to satisfy the equal part of "separate but equal." Huff has a section titled "James F. Byrnes and the Battle for Segregation that" includes a picture of a new Black school with the caption "Why were so many black schools built?" Huff's style, like the rest of his text, is rather boring, but he is willing to ask some direct questions about racism and occasionally offers quotations from white South Carolina leaders that are somewhat incriminating:

> He blamed "the politicians in Washington" and "Negro agitators in South Carolina" for the state's problems. He warned that South Carolina would "abandon the public school system" rather than desegregate (p. 404).

Jones begins his chapter "South Carolina Since 1945: Changing Social Patterns" with a photograph of African-American ministers marching in Orangeburg. He describes the realities of segregation and explains that court cases quickly brought important changes. This page has a photograph of Harvey Gantt and the caption tells us that he was the first Black student at Clemson and later the mayor of Charlotte. It might be added that Gantt lost a close senatorial race to Jesse Helms in the early 1990s and challenged him again in 1996. Jones's tone is slightly different in this chapter, but there are statements that are related to the general view of the text that absolves white South Carolinians for responsibility in race relations in the state. The following passage follows a paragraph on Martin Luther King and passive resistance:

> Passive resistance and the underlying threat of violence began to win speedy results in many places. It also antagonized many supporters of white supremacy whose reaction often resulted in widespread collisions, violence, and bloodshed.
>
> Not since the Civil War had the nation seemed so close to the brink of chaos. Amid all of the rioting of the 1960s, many fearfully saw the disrupted nation as approaching anarchy. The cords which held society together seemed to be snapping apart (p. 659).

The rest of the chapter is pretty straightforward with Jones taking the position of a cheerleader for both Black and white South Carolinians in his discussions of school integration and race relations in the state. Huff, of course, is also straightforward but he chooses to elaborate on the white forces that fought very hard against integration in the state. Governor Byrnes, Senator Thurmond, the Gressette committee, and Governor Timmerman's white supremist actions are discussed as is the legislature's passing a law for racially pure blood banks and the firing of University of South Carolina School of Education dean, Dr. Chester Travelstead for publically supporting school integration.

There are also differences in the author's treatment of school integration. Jones was very positive:

> When schools opened in the fall of 1970, all districts were at least "legally and technically" complying, and by the mid-1970s were complying generally and willingly. Utopia had not arrived—it rarely does. But sanity had been preserved. In some respects, it seemed like a miracle—like unscrambling an egg. It was an accomplishment which broke with the traditions 300 years old (p. 664).

This discussion is preceded by a photograph of local civil rights leader Modjeska Simkins (shown Governor Byrnes is on the same page) and followed by a section titled "Forces Working Toward Desegregation," which briefly discusses individuals and groups in the state who worked very hard for better race relations and the end of racism.

The Orangeburg Massacre (not so named in Jones's book) is discussed as part of a paragraph, but what is astounding is that there is no mention of the school integration battle in Clarendon County that was part of the *Brown* decision. Huff on the other hand discusses this battle for school integration and introduces Reverend DeLaine's heroic acts. However, he is not insensitive to successes and he gives credit to white South Carolinians when discussing Harvey Gantt enrolling in Clemson as well as the beginnings of school integration in Greenville. He acknowledges whites working for better race relations and tells the story of Governor Russell's 1963 Inaugural Barbecue for all South Carolinians—white and Black.

So while Jones's tone is less biased, the reality of racism by white South Carolinians is still avoided. Blacks are good if they go through the system quietly and whites in the state will come through in the end because they have good manners and morals. Consider this passage concerning the NAACP:

> It early made the important decision to concentrate the fighting in the courts and in a dialogue with the white power structure to avoid direct hostile and physical collision. News of that quiet dialogue began to come out only later. The results of seeking dialogue instead of confrontation were positive (p. 667).

Both Lewis P. Jones and Archie Vernon Huff Jr. provide their readers with a fairly extensive review of modern race relations in the state of South Carolina. Huff is again harder on white South Carolinians than Jones, but Jones does not avoid placing blame on white South Carolinians as much as he has in his discussions of slavery, Reconstruction, and Jim Crow. If Huff has a shortcoming in this section it is that he doesn't provide enough detail on the struggles of African-Americans in their fight for civil rights in South Carolina. While Jones is overly generous in his praise of white South Carolinians working for race relations, his major flaw is the omission of Reverend DeLaine and the battle for school integration in Clarendon County. Ironically, both Huff and Jones conclude by telling their readers how far we have come regarding race relations in both South Carolina and the rest of the nation. Without disputing progress and success, one wonders if Huff and Jones allow their young readers to finish both texts without questions about the segregation and racism that still exists in both South Carolina and the nation.

Conclusion

It probably goes too far to link portrayals of race in a sequence of history textbooks to race relations and white racism in South Carolina at the present time. On the other hand, the histories all these books recite the views that South Carolinians, past and present, hold on race.

Upon first consideration the textbooks discussed here appear similar to textbooks used in other states in their considerations of race. But this conclusion is complicated by the fact that race has been and still is a core issue for South Carolinians. A correspondence between turn-of-the-century and Simms–Oliphant South Carolina texts and American history textbooks appears if we consider Fitzgerald's analysis of the latter's work on race. The two South Carolina books currently used, however, fail to incorporate the changes that appeared in American history textbooks after 1970. This charge is truer of the Jones text, but is also true of Huff's book.

Fitzgerald found race seldom mentioned before the 1950s except in disparaging portrayals of slaves and Black reconstructionists. She offers the following depiction of slave life from the Barker, Dodd, and Commager text *Our Nation's Development*:

> Nor was the slave always unhappy in his cabin. On the contrary, he sang at his work. . . . If his cabin was small, there were shade trees about it, a vegetable garden near by and chickens in his coop (p. 83).

All of the South Carolina texts reviewed here, including the two texts used now, include similar depictions of slave life—except that the South Carolina texts make slave life seem even better and stress the love slaves held for their masters. Intuitively, one senses in the omission of both Blacks and a traditional analysis of race a continuing racism in South Carolina history textbooks. It is obvious and explicit in the treatment of race in the turn-of-the-century texts and the Simms-Oliphant texts and it is present by implication in both the Jones and Huff books.

Dargan and his contemporaries ignored Blacks except to belittle slaves and freedmen and included condescending descriptions of the "happy slave" and the ignorant freedman. They also ignored white racism and both condoned and glamorized white South Carolinians who oppressed Black people. The Simms–Oliphant textbooks, especially the editions before 1958, contain a similar orientation and tone. Newby placed the texts in a tradition that promoted white supremacy by either denigrating or ignoring Blacks as people and, disingenuously, ignoring white racism in South Carolina. In fact, the heroes set out for schoolchildren in South Carolina texts achieved fame for their white supremist acts. The post-Reconstruction hero Wade Hampton makes a perfect example. Newby discussed Hampton, with Calhoun and Tillman, as state heroes:

> Hampton might be the great white hero who 'redeemed' Carolina from Radical Reconstruction, but to black Carolinians 'redemption' was the end of a hopeful experiment in interracial democracy and the first step toward a counterrevolution of disfranchisement, white supremacy, and wholesale racial abuse (p. 11).

Newby's position in *Black Carolinians* is that both the general histories and the school histories in South Carolina were aimed to sustain and promote white supremacy. We have already read part of his analysis of Dargan. He is just as critical of Simms–Oliphant, and he concludes his analysis of both the turn-of-the-century texts and Simms-Oliphant with the following observation:

> they reveal a great deal about how the history of South Carolina was used as a tool of white supremacists. The history they presented was lily white. Most of them do not mention a single black by name; when blacks are discussed it is only in a disparaging context. Carolinians are white people. . . . The student, white or black, who absorbed and accepted the information in these books had no understanding of his

state or its people. He had instead a set of biases which interfered with a clear comprehension of past and present (p. 97).

Unfortunately, as regards to their treatment of race one can make the same statement about the last Simms-Oliphant book and the current texts. One might temper the assertion somewhat, but the basic message in both content and tone is the same. At worst, Jones's book is as mean spirited about Blacks and as condescending about slave life, and as myopic about all the outside influences that thwarted "good mannered and moral" white South Carolinians as both the turn-of-the century and Simms-Oliphant texts were. At best, Huff's book stands as a modernization of the classic Simms-Oliphant books. Huff, though, is less harsh in his treatment of Blacks and he is not an apologist for white atrocities. He is more honest than Jones and the preceding authors because he declines to excuse or condone white racism.

It is, of course, both fair and useful to judge historical analysis contextually within both the time and cultural setting of the work. In this case, some would argue that the turn-of-the-century texts, the Simms-Oliphant texts, and the current texts, are all captives of the periods in which they were written. Further, some would argue that no non-racist sources were available to turn of-the century writers and either Simms or Oliphant. Unfortunately for these arguments, William Sinclair's *The Aftermath of Slavery* and Frederick Douglass's *My Bondage and My Freedom* immediately come to mind. Meanwhile, the sources available to Jones and Huff are endless, and yet, Jones and to a lesser degree Huff choose to ignore them.

One thing that we can conclude from this review of South Carolina school history books is that they are racist. We know that they claim or imply that slaves were lucky to be captives in the United States. We know that they claim or imply that slaves were, on the one hand, adoring and loyal and, on the other hand, dangerous. We know that they claim or imply that abolitionists and any other "outsiders" opposed to slavery were malevolent. We know that they claim or imply that Radical Reconstruction was evil. We know that they claim or imply that the Ku Klux Klan was necessary for the survival of white South Carolinians. We know that the earlier texts claimed or implied that the Constitution of 1895 and its Black Codes were important for the survival of white South Carolina. We know that the later texts ignored twentieth century Black history in South Carolina. Finally, we know that none of the texts incorporated or incorporate the history of South Carolina's African Americans into their accounts of the state.

The question remains. How does the treatment of Blacks in South Carolina school history textbooks' relate to continuing white racism in the state? Do South Carolinians continue, like their textbooks, to blame outsiders and Blacks for their own racist acts? Do they deny their racism just as the texts deny the racism of the state's hallowed leaders—Calhoun, Hampton and Tillman; or our present day leaders; Thurmond, Hollings and Beasley? And how does this racism connect to the South Carolina histories children read in the past and read today? Although one can certainly argue that racism taints the textbooks and that white racism remains a regional and national disease, it is difficult to specify a definitive connection between the South Carolina school textbooks and the abiding racism. We do know that South Carolina school history textbooks themselves have a racist history and remain racist today. We also know that racism remains a reality in South Carolina and the rest of the nation. Finally, we know for a fact that it is time for racism to end. Erasing it from the South Carolina history textbooks should be easy enough, and enlightened textbooks can help to lessen lingering hate.

Chapter 11

The *Brown* Decision, Academic Freedom, and White Resistance: Dean Chester Travelstead and the University of South Carolina as a Case Study

Shortly after I began teaching at the University of South Carolina in 1986, a colleague from the University of Pittsburgh recalled his interview for a position in the College of Education at the university in 1972. He remembered an administrator telling him how the university handled "darkies." He accepted, instead, a position at Pitt. I think of his interview with some irony in that the university hired me precisely because of my research on race and education—more specifically school desegregation. My colleague's experience, however, reflects a white racist legacy that is an historical reality in South Carolina.

The University of South Carolina, itself, is part of the state's "heritage and tradition." One striking example of this tradition is the case of Dr. Chester Travelstead, Dean of the School of Education from 1953 through 1956. The university fired Travelstead in August of 1955 after he made a speech supporting the Supreme Court's ruling on school integration. This chapter examines the Travelstead case for the opportunity it presents to examine both the progress made in fighting racism and the persistence of racism.

When Chester Travelstead became the dean of education at the University of South Carolina, he was well aware of the state

government's official position on race and education as well
as the prosegregation sentiment of a high percentage of the
state's white population. Governor James Byrnes had become
an international figure as a senator, Supreme Court Justice
and the Secretary of State under Presidents Roosevelt and
Truman before returning home in 1950 to seek the governorship. Byrnes's position on school integration was clear, and
his major emphasis when he became governor was on a plan
called the "Educational Revolution," which entailed raising
large sums of money to finance new schools and school im-
provements throughout South Carolina. School districts were
consolidated from more than 1,200 to 102 and new schools
were built for both Blacks and whites. Governor Byrnes's (1958)
position was that neither Blacks nor whites wanted integrated
schools:

> . . . except for the professional agitators, what the colored people want,
> and what they are entitled to, is equal facilities in their schools. We
> must see that they get them (p. 408).

By contrast, a grassroots oral history of the struggle for desegregation in Clarendon County depicts rural Black South
Carolinians willing to sacrifice a great deal for integrated
schools. Lochbaum (1993) began a chapter entitled "Keeping
Lent" with this account:

> The word on the street was that the "negroes" wanted to send their
> children to the white schools with the white children. Perhaps this
> fear, which was nothing more than rumor at the time, was engen-
> dered by the knowledge of what they, the white people, would have
> wanted if it had been their children so situated (pp. 116–117).

Much earlier, southern historian I. A. Newby (1957) criticized Governor Byrnes's motives for his "Educational Revolution." In his classic book, *Black Carolinians*, and even earlier in
his master's thesis, "South Carolina and the Desegregation Issue: 1954–1956," Newby identified the Separate but Equal
Doctrine as the foundation of Governor Byrnes's position:

> Elected governor in 1950, he was inaugurated in January 1951. Al-
> most immediately the new governor began a long range program which
> was to provide a basis for the state's defense of the racial *status quo*
> and the *Plessy* doctrine of separate-but-equal schools. . . . South Caro-

lina, he announced, would not then "nor for some years to come mix white and colored children" in public schools. To prevent this the state would, if necessary, "reluctantly" abandon its public school system. "A lawful way" would be found to educate all children "and at the same time provide separate schools for the races" (pp. 36–37).

As a southerner, Dr. Travelstead understood the political reality regarding race in South Carolina and was perfectly familiar with the racist views of many South Carolinians. Born and raised in Kentucky, he became a school principal there in 1931. Before coming to South Carolina he served on the faculty at the University of Georgia. He arrived with no naiveté regarding race relations. When Chester Travelstead discussed his eventual firing, he explained that the president knew about his pro-integration viewpoint when he offered him the deanship of the School of Education:

> In the early summer of 1953, I discussed with Pres. Donald Russell of the University of South Carolina the possibility of Negroes being admitted to the university, and he said at the time that he fully expected Negroes to apply for admission and to be admitted in "two or three years." Having been a member of the faculty at the University of Georgia where a Negro had been denied admission to the Law School because of his race, I told Pres. Russell I felt keenly that such denials should not and could not continue in graduate schools of southern universities in the face of previous U.S. Supreme Court decisions to the contrary. He agreed and three days later employed me as dean of the university's School of Education (p. 144).

Recall here that Russell, himself, had to have understood the Governor's and the state legislature's position regarding integration. That viewpoint did not change with the *Brown* decision and Governor Byrnes's successor, George Bell Timmerman Jr. (1955), made his position quite clear in his inaugural address:

> The other is the gravest problem that we as a government and we as individuals have faced in modern times. It is the impending threat of compulsory social mixing of white and Negro children in our public schools (pp. 7–8).

Timmerman then praised Governor Byrnes's "Educational Revolution," condemned the decisions of the Supreme Court, and pleaded for parents to protect their right to segregated schools for their children:

White parents do not wish their children to mix in public schools
with large groups of Negro children. Most Negro parents do not want
their children to mix with large groups of white children. These pa-
rental objections are alone sufficient and should be respected . . . but
when Negroes combine against whites, it is inevitable that whites will
combine against Negroes and both races will suffer. Loyal South Carolinians will stand firm against any organized effort to destroy the right
of parents to choose what is best for their children (p. 9).

Timmerman devoted much of his governorship to supporting nullification and interposition, and he promoted a "states'
rights" third party. Subsequent speeches on race repeated these
opinions and added condemnation for northern whites, Black
"agitators," and the NAACP, all of whom he characterized as
communists.

Timmerman's April 1955 speech to the South Carolina Education Association finally persuaded Dean Travelstead to state
his views on integration publicly. Travelstead had become
troubled by the fact that no public voice even moderately challenged the general opposition to the Supreme Court's decision in *Brown*. He wrote a letter to the governor protesting
statements in his speech to the association. He sent his letter
on personal stationary, responding specifically to
Timmerman's points. The governor had said that the Supreme
Court decision meant "for the first time in judicial history that
equality of treatment is discrimination." Dean Travelstead answered that the *Brown* decision neither said nor implied this
but rather stated "that segregation is in and of itself discrimination and therefore a violation of the Fourteenth Amendment"
(p. 145).

Timmerman also questioned the character of integrationists, saying that they were "men of talent and little character."
Travelstead questioned Timmerman's evidence and offered a
counterpoint: "It is my opinion that many men of great stature
are sincerely convinced that the May 17 ruling of the Supreme
Court was both timely and sound" (p. 145).

Dean Travelstead appeared to be especially troubled by the
following statement:

No precedent, no parallel, can be found for compulsory integration.
It is new. It is novel. It is contrary to the divine order of things. Only
an evil mind can conceive it. Only a foolish mind can accept it
(p. 145).

Travelstead responded that public schools have always integrated students "who differ widely in educational, social, mental, emotional, physical, and cultural backgrounds and achievements, and we are faced with extreme differences— whether within one race or among different races" (p. 145). He explained that thirty-one states and the District of Columbia already had racially integrated schools, and he challenged Timmerman's rhetoric in referring to integrationists as evil-minded and foolish-minded. Finally, Dean Travelstead asked the governor how he could justify breaking the law of the land and asked what kind of message his behavior might send to schoolchildren (p. 145).

Chester Travelstead never received a response, but he did receive a call from the president of the university. Once President Russell had read the letter the two men met on June 1, 1955. Travelstead described the meeting in his 1956 *School and Society* article: "He was not pleased that I had written the letter, but he did not direct or even suggest that I desist from writing about or discussing the matter of segregation" (p. 145). Shortly afterward, Russell reappointed Travelstead and gave him a pay raise.

But the story then changed quickly. On August 2, 1955, Travelstead delivered a speech to four hundred students and faculty members in the School of Education. The speech, entitled "Today's Decisions for Tomorrow's Schools," included a discussion of school integration. The dean lamented the silence of those educators and professional organizations in South Carolina who might support integration, and he also addressed the morality of racial equality. The following excerpt portrays Travelstead's tone:

> It is my firm conviction that enforced segregation of the races in our public schools can no longer be justified on any basis and should, therefore, be abolished as soon as practicable. Even though, as a white southerner, I have since my early childhood, taken for granted the practice of segregation, I can find now no justification for it (p. 146).

Dean Travelstead took a short vacation and when he returned to his home on August 21, 1955, he found a letter (later it appeared in the student newspaper *The Gamecock*, December

2, 1955 under the byline of C. McClung) from the secretary of
the university's board of trustees notifying him of his dismissal:

> The Executive Committee of the Board of Trustees is of the opinion
> that it is not in the best interest of the University to renew your ap-
> pointment as dean of the school of education. It wishes, however, to
> give you the benefit of appropriate notice of termination. Therefore
> you are advised that your services will end at the conclusion of the
> fiscal year 1955–56 (p. 2).

Travelstead met with President Russell two days later and his
report of the meeting was of being informed that "the University would be embarrassed before the legislature" by pro-integration statements (p. 146). The board of trustees held a hearing at Dean Travelstead's request on October 27, 1955. There
was discussion of both Dr. Travelstead's letter to Governor
Timmerman and his speech to students and faculty at the hearing. Travelstead subsequently discussed the hearing with *The
Gamecock*.

> At this meeting I was given the impression that the Executive Com-
> mittee was of the opinion: 1. That persons employed by the univer-
> sity should not engage in discussions of controversial issues. One
> member did say, however, that if I had made a pro-segregation speech
> on August 2, instead of the one I did make, he would have approved
> of it (p. 2).

As far as the university was concerned, the case was closed.
The executive committee of the board of trustees had acted
promptly and efficiently and even "mannerly" in dismissing
Dean Travelstead. Travelstead accepted a position in mid-
November as the dean of education at the University of New
Mexico, which began in February, 1956.

   Shortly after accepting his new position, however, Dr.
Travelstead spoke with the local press regarding his dismissal,
and his story drew newspaper responses throughout the state
and nation. The extreme positions came from the *Charleston
News and Courier* (November 25, 1955) and the *Florence Morning News* (November 26, 1955). The Florence paper headed its
coverage "To Stifle Controversy Is to Kill the University," the
first three words serving as an explanation for Dr. Travelstead's
firing. The Charleston article wholeheartedly supported the
firing:

> Dr. Travelstead, in opposing segregation of the races in public schools,
> is out of line both with the university and with the desires of the
> people of South Carolina. . . . His usefulness as a teacher of educa-
> tion in this state is therefore over.

It was the *The Gamecock*, however, that provided the most extensive coverage of Dean Travelstead's dismissal. Five articles
as well as a letter to the editor appeared in the December 2,
1955, edition, one article and letters appeared on December
9, and more continued to appear through January of 1956. All
of the articles in the December 2, issue supported Dean
Travelstead's right to make his speech and condemned the
university for his dismissal. The newspaper's lead article,
"Travelstead Says Board Fired Him," written by Carolyn
McClung, for the most part repeated Travelstead's account of
the events that led to his firing. McClung, Herbert Bryant, and
Drew James also wrote articles questioning the university's role
as a censor.

The issue in all three articles was academic freedom, not
school integration or white racism, although McClung did not
separate the two:

> If university officials take it upon themselves to squelch people with
> ideas not coinciding with their own, then it is no place for students
> with intellectual curiosity. However, the Board of Trustees as far as
> we can determine, has never issued such a statement, but it is evident
> that integration is one subject which should not be discussed (p. 2).

The only article that specifically addressed Travelstead's
position on school integration (in the December 2, edition of
The Gamecock) was written by Jack Bass, who has enjoyed a
long and successful career in journalism and has often written
on racism in the South. For example he later co-authored with
Jack Nelson *The Orangeburg Massacre*, the story of the state
police killing four students at South Carolina State College in
Orangeburg, South Carolina, in 1968. Bass's article in *The
Gamecock*, "Travelstead Speech Found Intelligent," applauded
Dean Travelstead for a reasoned analysis of South Carolina's
"segregation problem" and condemned the university for dismissing the dean for his rational and moral position. Bass es-
timated that 90 percent of the faculty at the university agreed
with Travelstead.

An article in the paper's next issue as well as many of the letters to the editor took issue with Bass's position. Billy Mellette's article, "Travelstead—We Are in South Carolina," is a folksy essay on how whites and Blacks got along in South Carolina before the NAACP arrived. It argued that Dean Travelstead got what he deserved:

> South Carolina is pro-segregation. The Legislature, reflecting that and consequently pro-segregation, shows the school the way in which they should go. It is only reasonable they should go that way. Like it or not, we are South Carolinians. . . . Let us face it: The University officials would not have knocked on Mr. Travelstead's door and told him to quit if he hadn't said something not in keeping with their policy. If he did not know to be quiet—as head of the education department, of all positions— then he has now learned, and the school has told the world where they stand. The University did not invade the castle of free thought. It was challenged and forced to commit itself, no matter how reasonable and how mild Mr. Travelstead made his declaration. There are not many Negroes in New Mexico (p. 6).

The majority of letters to the editor more or less agreed with Mellette and opposed Bass and *The Gamecock*'s defenders of academic freedom. Most of the letters chastised Travelstead for a position repugnant to the citizens of South Carolina. On December 9, one writer named LeClerq supported Travelstead's right to his opinion while questioning his right "to occupy a position through which he could mold the opinions of prospective teachers of a state where race purity and segregation are essential to the well being of its citizens" (p. 6). This writer, as well as others, equated integrationists with communists and found it the university's duty to dismiss Dean Travelstead.

Some letters supported the paper's stand on academic freedom and one letter, written on December 2, tongue-in-cheek, *The Gamecock* mistakenly interpreted as supporting the board of trustees. The editors headed it "Texan Applauds Trustees":

> It is quite evident that those concepts of Freedom, which Dr. Travelstead possesses, are of the utmost DANGER to the principles and traditions of the South. . . . His influence on these future educators might have resulted in their recognition of equality of rights and the freedom of opinion as the keys to both progress and world peace. Such opinion is reality, therefore, in the interest of the past and for the preservation of those so-related practices, the board of "little white

gods" could have made no other choice than that decision which they
so proudly rendered (p. 2).

Travelstead wrote a letter to the newspaper in January but it
dealt with academic freedom rather than race. He left for his
new position at the University of New Mexico and a new dean
was appointed by the middle of February. I. A. Newby, cited
earlier, and Harry Golden, the famous southern Jewish editor
of *The Carolina Israelite*, severely criticized the university's dismissal of Travelstead. Golden concluded his editorial, reprinted
in his 1960 book *Enjoy, Enjoy*, by lamenting South Carolina's
loss:

> Thus, South Carolina lost one of its ablest educators, the rest of the
> faculty was effectively silenced, and the University of South Carolina
> became a beleaguered fortress of academic freedom in what Gover-
> nor Timmerman called "The War of Northern Aggression" (p. 208).

Harry Golden's remarks provide an appropriate eulogy for
the Travelstead case and a neat synopsis of the historical reality of racism and the post–*Brown* resistance to school integration in South Carolina. Public schools were legally integrated
in the state in 1963 but not without extended and active resistance and a proliferation of private schools that have been
properly referred to throughout the state as "segregationist
academies." Although many of these academies no longer stand
as bastions of segregation and public schools throughout the
state are legally integrated, the appearance and the reality often diverge. Suburban schools that were initially destinations
for those seeking to avoid school integration are reasonably
integrated at the present time. By contrast, in urban South
Carolina and in the state's pockets of rural Black poverty, the
schools remain segregated. For example, Scotts Branch School
in Clarendon County, a school that was joined in the *Brown*
decision, had a student population during the 1993-94 school
year that included only one white student.

The student body at the University of South Carolina was
also integrated in 1963 when three African-Americans—Henri
Montieth, Robert Anderson, and James L. Solomon—enrolled
there. Some 15 percent of the current student population is
African-American. Thus, human struggle has brought some
change to South Carolina in race relations. Chester Travelstead

would hardly be fired for challenging racism in 1994. Still, public expressions of racism in the state in recent years tend to attract as much support as condemnation. More important, the school segregation Dr. Travelstead challenged remains a South Carolina reality.

The firing of Dean Travelstead is not a proud moment in the history of the university or the state of South Carolina. It is important, though, for South Carolinians to acknowledge and remember it because it is part of the common heritage. By according it credence one recognizes the honest progress made on race relations in South Carolina and one begins to address the racism that still exists.

Chapter 12

South Carolina and Me: Children, Diversity, But Still Opression

The photo essay that follows portrays the schizophrenic reality of life in South Carolina as we approach the 21st century. *Money Magazine* rates Columbia as one of the places in the nation most conducive to African-American social mobility. Yet pockets of both urban and rural poverty in South Carolina rival the impoverishment of Third World nations. Suburban white and Black children often attend school together while urban and rural schools remain racially segregated, including Scotts Branch School which in 1954 was joined in the *Brown* v *Topeka* decision. Some Blacks and whites serve on integrated commissions, belong to the same clubs, and attend the same churches. But other clubs and churches remain adamantly segregated even if it is *de facto* rather than *de jure*. While some teachers promote equality and teach Martin Luther King's "I Have a Dream" speech, others use South Carolina history texts that still blame present racial inequality on the abolitionists of the last century and the civil rights movement of the 1960s. Moreover—and symbolically significant—the state still flies the confederate flag atop its Capitol and in the Redneck Shop in Laurens the self-proclaimed white supremacist openly sells Ku Klux Klan paraphernalia.

All of these polarities are part of the current South Carolina scene. The hopes and possibilities appear in the portraits of the children: portraits of ethnic and socioeconomic diversity, portraits of children who in spite of the current contradictions will know each other more as equals than those who preceded them did. The agents of oppression, though, retain their menace. A local rabbi recently told me that the KKK was no longer a threat and he no longer had to concern himself with neo-Nazis. Although I pray he is correct, I think it is still wise to be wary of the hatred and threats of oppression that remain possible.

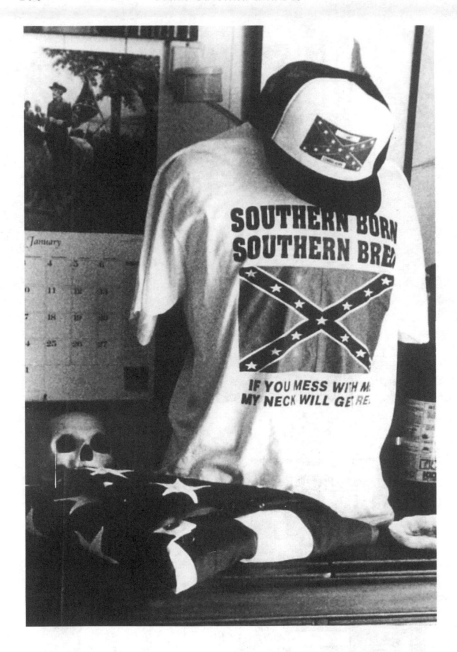

SECTION FOUR

INTRODUCTORY NOTE

This section features a concluding chapter on Afrocentrisms written in the early nineties amid the controversy surrounding the Portland Baseline Essays on the African and African-American curricula, the New York State curriculum on multiculturalism, and the broader debate on Afrocentrism as a world view. I wrote this counterpoint article to suggest Afrocentrism as a way to promote racial equality and harmony for all Americans. It concludes this book because I believe it offers a route toward racial progress.

Chapter 13

Afrocentrisms: Capitalist, Democratic, and Liberationist Portraits

Introduction

Afrocentrism and the Afrocentric curriculum receive growing attention in the educational press. Since roughly November of 1990, numerous articles on the subjects have appeared in, for example *Education Week*, *The Chronicle of Higher Education*, and *The Educational Excellence Network News and Views*. The discussion has included even-handed pro and con articles as well as outright attacks on Afrocentrism and the Afrocentric curriculum. Whether fair or heavy-handed, the articles all tend to view the issue from the perspective of the horror story. The three most familiar criticisms are that the movement (1) embodies historical distortion, (2) promotes a divisive curriculum, or (3) represents a race-driven curriculum.

At their worst, the critics portray Afrocentrists as people who consider African and African-American all good and European-American and white all bad. Afrocentrists are viewed as people who want to "take over" the school curriculum and make Afrocentrism the official American curriculum (Innerst, 1990; Sullivan, 1990; Duin, 1990; and Leo, 1990).

This chapter takes exception to these analyses. Its purpose is to present examples of Afrocentrism tending toward African and African-American "inclusion" and "infusion" in the school curriculum. As the chapter proceeds, it becomes evident why the title of this essay is "Afrocentrisms." Although the criticisms of Afrocentrism are monolithic, the Afrocentrist movement is diverse. Conservatives, liberals, and radicals all find accommodation, as do capitalists, socialists, and communists. Afrocentrism is a broad movement that promotes the inclusion of a broad spectrum of African and African-American history and culture in the school curriculum. Accordingly, it defies a neat definition.

The current Afrocentric movement has been shaped by three events: the meetings of The Conference for the Infusion of African and African-American Content in the High School Curriculum held in Atlanta in 1989 and 1990; the publication of the *African-American Baseline Essays* by the Portland Public Schools in 1989; and the publication of the New York State Minority Task Force's *A Curriculum of Inclusion* in 1989. Each of these events provided broad conceptions and theories of Afrocentrism and the Afrocentric curriculum. This chapter examines, as I said, a variety of Afrocentrisms. The Afrocentric portraits presented here connect African and African-American history and culture to the continuing fight against racism in American society and American education. It includes analyses of three strains of Afrocentrism: (1) capitalist Afrocentrism, (2) democratic Afrocentrism, and (3) liberationist Afrocentrism.

The most often cited conceptualization of Afrocentrism appears in Molefi Kete Asante's 1987 book, *The Afrocentric Idea.* Chairman of African-American studies at Temple University, Philadelphia, Asante begins by distinguishing African and African-American history and culture from European and European-American history and culture. The former stresses humanism and communalism; the latter stresses materialism. Asante asserts that the beliefs and behaviors of African-Americans should be portrayed and understood within the context of African and African-American history and culture. He cites a variety of African and African-American scholars and white scholars like Martin Bernal and Michael Bradley as willing and prepared to explore Afrocentrism. He presents the nobility of African roots as a worthy foundation for the education of African-Americans today. The work of three other Afrocentrist educators—Janice Hale-Benson, Ramona Edelin, and Booker Peek—represent the three principal Afrocentrist views mentioned earlier: capitalist, democratic, and liberationist. Additional representations of Afrocentrism appear throughout this chapter, but it focuses mainly on the work of Hale-Benson, Edelin, and Peek because each views Afrocentrism as the connecting of African and African-American history and culture to the continuing struggle against racism and for civil rights.

Capitalist Afrocentrism

Some Afrocentrists would view Afrocentrism and capitalism as contradictory views of the world. Other Africans and African-Americans, both past and present, have advanced beliefs and adopted behaviors that support the co-existence of capitalism and African history and culture. An African-American colleague of mine, an early childhood education professor, has characterized Hale-Benson as "speaking out of both sides of her mouth." The analysis was more objective than judgmental. At first, Afrocentrism and capitalism appear to be strange bedfellows. Nevertheless, this partnership can illuminate the problems and issues connected to the relationship of education, work, and race. The educational issues, and subsequently the occupational issues, that Hale-Benson's program, "Visions for Children" addresses constitute a reaction to the racism and inequality that still exist in American society. Hale-Benson reviewed her visions for children in Kofi Lomotey's collection, *Going to School: The African-American Experience* (1990), a book of diverse essays "geared toward the formulation and implementation of practices and policies designed to improve the academic achievement of African-American students" (p. xiii).

Capitalistic Afrocentrism confronts the racial disparity that exists in American education and society at the present time. In *Going to School*, James Comer, an African-American professor of psychology at Yale, introduces the need for an educational approach that acknowledges and acts on "the socioeconomically disadvantaged condition of Black children and the failure of educational institutions to respond appropriately and humanistically to the needs created by these conditions" (p. 103). Statistically, these conditions include (1) a 45-percent dropout rate among urban Blacks, (2) a 72-percent dropout rate among urban Black males, (3) a 3-times-greater chance for a Black child than a white child to be poor, (4) a median income for Black families at 57.1 percent of the income for white families, (5) a 4-times-greater chance for Black mothers than white mothers to die in childbirth and (6) a 15.2-percent unemployment rate for Blacks as against a 6-percent rate for whites.

Hale-Benson's work addresses the racial disparity with a program that stresses the need for the bicultural education of African-American children. She introduces biculturalism within the context of W. E. B. Dubois's early work on "the talented tenth," where he explained that Blacks lived in two worlds: the world of African heritage and culture, and the world of white culture. Both required acknowledgment, and although Dubois later hedged on his theory, Hale-Benson builds "Visions for Children" on the same premise. Hale-Benson's program combines a curriculum of African-American culture and heritage with a curriculum of information and skills that promotes "upward mobility, career achievement, and financial independence in the American mainstream" (*Going to School*, p. 212). African and African-American studies are integrated in a curriculum that stresses language and communication skills, cognitive skills, and mathematical skills, as well as an enhanced self-concept and positive attitudes toward learning and school. African and African-American history and culture are taught along with standard English. African and African-American oral tradition, art, and music are an ongoing part of the curriculum, as is the study of African diaspora communities and such holidays as those honoring the Emancipation Proclamation, Dr. Martin Luther King Jr. Day, Juneteenth, Malcolm X's Birthday, Kwanza, and the 14th Amendment to the Constitution. Hale-Benson cites Hakim Rashid for theoretical support of herbicultural curriculum beginning at the pre-school level:

> To achieve equal educational outcomes for Black children, it will be necessary to design an educational system that complements rather than opposes Black culture. The preschool experience must therefore provide a dynamic blend of African-American culture and that culture which is reflected in the Euro-American educational setting. The African-American child who only sees the Euro-American cultural tradition manifested in the preschool environment can only conclude that the absence of visual representation of his culture connotes his essential worthlessness (p. 210).

Hale-Benson's "Visions for Children" program includes training for teachers so that they become sensitive to building self-concepts and positive school attitudes. The emphasis, however, appears to be on the skills needed for upward mobility set within the context of self-concept and Afrocentrism. Hale-Benson explains that the early nurturing of reading and writing skills directly influence college admission tests, and she is emphatic about standard English: "One fact is clear: speaking standard English is a skill needed by Black children for upward mobility" (p. 216).

"Visions for Children" is a program that nurtures Hale-Benson's biculturalism. African and African-American history and culture provide positive educational reinforcement and combine with standard educational excellence to celebrate ethnicity as well as educational and occupational upward mobility. Hale-Benson's vision is what Cameron McCarthy (1990) disparagingly refers to as "a multicultural emancipatory program" (p. 48.) He includes Bullivant and Rushton among the proponents of programs that foster ethnic history and culture to help minority students advance educationally and occupationally. Then he recruits Crichlow, Troyna, and Williams to critique multicultural emancipatory theory. He considers it naive and unresponsive to the existing reality of class disparity and racism that still prevails in American society. But Hale-Benson is well aware of the present reality; moreover, if one extends McCarthy's critique, one might conclude that the expected payoffs of "Visions for Children" are antithetical to the realities of American education and society.

Democratic Afrocentrism

Two of the essays in the *African-American Baseline Essays*, Michael Harris on art and Joyce Braden Harris on language arts, address the democratic heritage of African and African-American culture. The collective nature of African art is stressed, as are present examples of democratic African-American art cooperatives where much of the work is political in nature, with the message of racial equality. Joyce Harris explores democratic Afrocentrism through the African oral tradition—a tradition now celebrated by African-Americans:

Black speech has a collective orientation based on African communal values. Speakers who are able to use the rhythm of the ancestors to verbalize the Black condition become folk heroes to African-Americans (Portland Baseline Essays).

Joyce Harris cites Martin Luther King's "I Have a Dream" speech and Jesse Jackson's speech at the 1987 Democratic Convention as examples. One of the more thoughtful explorations of Democratic Afrocentrism came from Ramona Edelin's presentation at the Atlanta Conference (1989). Edelin's speech, "Curriculum and Cultural Identity," is a proposal for an Afrocentric curriculum that reasserts the African-American democratic cultural integrity of the past and encourages African-American participation and involvement in educational policy and decision making.

Edelin is informed by W.E.B. Dubois's *The Gift of Black Folk: Negroes in the Making of America*, which celebrated the "unyielding democratic spirit" of African-Americans. She calls for an African-American reassertion of this spirit:

> The African American group lacks cultural integrity, and has started a process of self-correction and consensus-building for the specific purpose of rectifying this serious problem. In many important respects, our forebears who were slaves, sharecroppers, and servants enjoyed a higher degree of cultural integrity than we do today. They founded schools, businesses, and mutual aid societies together; their values and their devotion to duty were rock steady; they made time to help and care for one another and to enforce and pass on their beliefs, intentions, ways of doing things, traditions and group vision. They resisted systemic assaults on their dignity and humanity; and they perpetuated and advanced our group (pp. 39–40).

Edelin is not romanticizing the past, but rather calling for group action in the present. Her vision corresponds well with Richard Long, whose Atlanta presentation addressed the need for intense African-American cultural education for all African-Americans under thirty years old. For Edelin, a Democratic Afrocentric education well serves young African-Americans. Her call for participation and involvement in educational policy both addresses the societal problems currently affecting young African-Americans and advocates the abandonment of theories like "cultural deprivation" that erode the possibilities of educational excellence for African-American children. Edelin believes that the African-American democratic heritage can reduce teen-age pregnancy and eradicate drugs from the lives of African-American youth. She also believes that the African-American democratic heritage can lend valuable substance to the Afrocentric school curriculum.

Edelin's Democratic Afrocentrism amounts to a reconceptualization of both the character and the content of school curriculum. Because it is democratic rather than capitalistic, and because it is informed by the communal, collective nature of the African and African-American heritage, Edelin's Afrocentrism does not settle for just a "piece of the American pie" (as if one had been offered!). She explains emphatically, "No! As we have said many times, in many contexts, once we get into the mainstream, the mainstream will change" (p. 43). That change was presaged by Dubois, this time his book, *Black Reconstruction*. It is a change that asks for "absolute equality" and thus "the advance of all humanity"(p. 45).

Liberationist Afrocentrism

Cameron McCarthy (1990) draws upon Marvin Berlowitz's work and places white racism in America within the context of class analysis as an issue that "must be understood in the proper perspective as forms of ideological mystification designed to facilitate exploitation and weaken the collective power of the labouring classes"(p. 49). Afrocentrist educators hardly deny the reality of class disparity in American society, but their vision of liberation begins with white racism rather than class theory. This assumption is evident in the work of Booker Peek, an Oberlin College professor who eschews scholarly writing, tutors children and adults in northern Ohio, and directs his college students in the same work with the purpose of achieving African-American liberation. As Lomotey (1990) describes it, Peek's analysis of racism and disparate educational and economic achievement begins with the premise that "the discrepancy is attributable to the fact there is a racism that has been keeping Blacks in inferior positions, and making Blacks themselves feel inferior" (p. 21). Both aspects of Peek's premise are important for an analysis of Liberationist Afrocentrism.

Peek divides liberationist Afrocentrism into two formats: political education and skills education. Political education encompasses all of our lives; it just depends on whether it is a political education we choose or one others choose for us. As Lomotey noted, political education includes culture, history, desire, and aspirations:

> For Black Americans it has to be a total quest for liberation not only for ourselves but for all oppressed people throughout the world—particularly those in Africa. That's political education. So, I see a need for involving children with cultural education. That comes under political education and is the responsibility of parents and of family and anyone else who cares about the political development of the child. There is no way to eliminate that possibility; you will either be politically educated to represent and respond to your own needs and desires or you will be responding to the needs and desires of other people (p. 15).

Peek's definition of political education argues compellingly for the infusion and inclusion of Afrocentric education in the school curriculum. It is an extension of Edelin's argument presented earlier, but it goes further by directly connecting political education and skills education. While skills education is neutral, in his Oberlin work Peek equates skills and tools and considers such preparation essential for African-American liberation. Afrocentricity is part of liberation, but it is meaningless without skills education. African and African-American history and culture are important, but they are impotent if they fail to connect to the current African-American reality. If they do connect—the example being the political education Peek considers essential—then Afrocentrism will initiate the demand of skills education among African-Americans.

Lomotey recalls Peek discussing the marriage of political and skills education within the context of the two issues just introduced: white racism in American society, and a resignation to inferiority among African-Americans. He also recalls Peek addressing the work of Jensen and Shockley, tracking, the self-fulfilling prophecy, and the recent resurgence of overt racism in the United States. Here is Lomotey reciting Peek's general indictment:

> I would say that the state of Black education is directly attributable to the social conditions in the society, starting with our enslavement—physical enslavement—and continuing up to now with our psychological enslavement where we don't quite have the same kinds of standards for our liberation or define it as do most other people; that's

total and absolutely unquestionable liberation. In that sense, I would say the totality of Black education is affected by the social system (p. 14).

Peek analyzes Jensen and Shockley's work in two different ways. Initially, he explains that neither their arguments nor evidence are compelling, especially within a society and an educational system that still discriminate on the basis of color. Jensen and Shockley are also problematic precisely because their views are still accepted, though often quietly, by American educators. This is evident in Peek's further discussion of Black education and what educators refer to as the "self-fulfilling prophecy":

> Now, once that philosophy remains in place, then children are not taught properly. They are not taught by teachers who believe in them so they don't learn to read, and they don't learn to write because in school reading and writing and thinking critically are the tools that are offered. . . . Students are turned off. It's boring. . . . Reading and writing and thinking are activities that are extremely boring if you can't do them—if you don't have people who believe that you can do them and that you must do them (p. 19).

Peek also connects tracking to this discussion. Modern day tracking is self-tracking. Black students do not choose chemistry, physics, or honor courses because they have never been provided with the prerequisite skills education.

The most powerful part of the white racism argument is the reference to its resurgence. Peek views high drop-out rates, low high school graduation rates, and diminishing enrollments of African-Americans at the university level as concomitant issues of white power, itself an attempt to return to a 1950s image of white supremacy by keeping the number of Black professionals low. The argument, of course, becomes more potent when one witnesses the increasingly overt white racism on college campuses. Peek told Lomotey that the greatest tragedy is that "the evils that whites perpetuated initially have carried over into us today to the extent that we are participating in the conspiracy" (p. 17).

At the heart of Liberationist Afrocentrism is the work of African-Americans in promoting political education, history and culture, and demanding skills education:

we must start seeing it as abnormal that we do not perform in reading, writing, and arithmetic as well as the dominant culture. We must
see that as abnormal. We have to see that a change must be under-
taken regardless of the cost or time. If we are unable to do that, we
will remain in an inferior position. But if we are able to alter our
political education, what would follow would be a strong desire to
acquire skills education which is offered in school systems and in
homes, and we would not accept the low level performance which is
typical for the majority of Black Americans. That would change everything (p. 18).

Peek places the burden on African-American educators,
teachers and professors, as well as African-American professionals. He insists that they be outraged by both white racism
and African-American inferiority in skills education. It is time,
he thinks, for African-Americans to demand equality and quality education. His tutoring provides a personal example—
neither social class nor race need determine ability or learning capacity. In fact, he considers skills education an easy proposition:

what I am saying is whether one is reared in an upper-middle-class
home or not, once the parents understand and the school systems
understand that education can be supplemented by nearly 3,000 or
4,000 additional words, that child in that environment will suddenly
have what would be considered an upper-middle-class education mi-
nus the social things that would go with that particular education
(p. 20).

Peek also stresses the institutional responsibility of schools
and teachers for providing uneducated parents with this knowledge and their children with a quality skills education. He continually stresses the responsibility of African-American educators and professionals in particular, he discusses white racism
in terms of white power, and he acknowledges that quality skills
education fails to reach a high percentage of white Americans.
It is right out of C. Wright Mills's work, both *White Collar* and
The Power Elite. More pressing for Peek is the cooptation of
middle-class African-Americans. Are individual suburban
homes and professional jobs antithetical to both a political
and skills education for all African-Americans? This question
is, of course, beginning to receive extensive attention. Roger
Wilkin's work on neoconservative Blacks has been joined by
William Julius Wilson's *The Truly Disadvantaged* and Nicholas

Lemann's study of Chicago (Wilkens, 1986; Wilson, 1986; Lemann, 1991). Peek acknowledges the reality and then demands its reversal. Liberationist Afrocentrism requires a quality education for all African-Americans.

Finally, Peek turns Liberationist Afrocentrism into a life-and-death issue for all Americans. The education of the few equates with the belief that "might makes right." A belief in quality education for all means a belief in the productivity and essential decency of all humanity. The former is genocidal, the latter is life affirming for African-Americans, for European-Americans, for all Americans.

Conclusion

This chapter portrays three different examples of Afrocentrism. The three different portraits, however, share a common thread. Each asserts the need for the connection of Afrocentrism or African and African-American history and culture to the struggle against racism and for equality that continues today in the United States of America. Each of the Afrocentrisms presented here promotes a different outcome, or "payoff" if you like. For Janice Hale-Benson it is an Afrocentrism that can promote the "American Dream" for African-American children. Ramona Edelin's Afrocentrism can reawaken the African and African-American communal orientation to promote democracy in the United States and throughout the world. Booker Peek's Afrocentrism promotes educational and occupational excellence for all—African-Americans, European-Americans, and the entire brotherhood of man and woman.

The point to stress one last time is that this is a story of Afrocentrisms. Each is a form of Afrocentrism, and each is different. None of the three is exclusive. None promotes the exclusion of white people. Each assumes a world of inclusion. One could have presented other Afrocentrisms but the three portrayed here were chosen for their diversity and for their educational possibilities.

Although I might prefer some combination of Edelin and Peek to Hale-Benson, the truth is we have no idea what results an Afrocentric curriculum—whether it follow one of these three portraits or others—will produce. Peek's thoughts on skills education, reminiscent of Martin Buber and Bernard Mehl, provide an appropriate concluding thought. Peek speaks of skills education, but delete skills for the moment: "Education may allow a person to live a life like Hitler or a life like Mother Teresa." One cannot keep a scorecard. The Afrocentrism Edelin and Peek offer is an Afrocentrism of possibilities. The outcome is uncertain, but the alternatives are intolerable.

References

Anderson, E. (1990). *Streetwise: Race, Class and Change in an Urban Community*. Chicago: University of Chicago Press.

Asante, M. K. (1987). *The Afrocentric Idea*. Philadelphia: Temple University Press.

Bass, J. "Travelstead Speech Found Intelligent." *The Gamecock*, December 2, 1955, p. 2.

Beatty, J. "Race, Class and the City," *Atlantic Monthly*, September 1985.

Becker, H. (1981). *Exploring Society Photographically*. Chicago: University of Chicago Press.

Buber, M. (1970). *I and Thou*. New York: Scribner.

Byrnes, J. (1958). *All in One Lifetime*. New York: Harper & Brothers.

Chapman, J. (1895). *School History of South Carolina*. Richmond: Everett Waddey.

Coles, R. (1972). *Farewell to the South*. Boston: Little, Brown.

Coles, R. (1967). *The South Goes North*. Boston: Little, Brown.

Coles, R. "Boston's Anguish: Race, Class, and Schools," *Washington Monthly*, September 8, 1985.

Coles, R. (1967) *Children of Crisis*. Boston: Little, Brown.

Coles, R. (1964a). "How Do Teachers Feel?" *Saturday Review*, May 16, pp. 72–73.

Comer, J., & Haynes, N. (1990). "Helping Black Children Succeed: The Significance of Some Social Factors," in *Going to School*.

Crain, R., & Mahard, R. (1978). "School Racial Composition and Black College Attendance and Achievement Test Performance. *Sociology of Education*, 51.

Crain, R. (1969). *The Politics of School Desegregation*. Chicago: Aldine.

Cruse, H. (1987). *Plural But Equal*. New York: Morrow.

Dargan, J. (1906). *School History of South Carolina*. Columbia, SC: The State Company.

deLone, R. (1978). *Small Futures*. New York: Harcourt, Brace, Jovanovich.

Dubois, W. E. B. (1903). *The Souls of Black Folk*. Chicago: McClurg.

Duin, S. "A Return to Segregationsist History," *The Oregonian*. November 11, 1990.

Edelin, R. (1989) "Curriculum and Cultural Identity," in *Infusion of African and African-American Content in the School Curriculum*.

Edwards, H. (1980). *The Struggle That Must Be*. New York: Macmillan.

Elkins, S. (1968). *Slavery*. Chicago: University of Chicago Press.

Fitzgerald, F. (1979). *America Revised: History Schoolbooks in the Twentieth Century*. Boston: Little, Brown.

Genovese, E. (1974). *Roll Jordan Roll*. New York: Pantheon.

Gewen, B. "A City Without a Middle," *The New Leader*, November 4, 1985.

Golden, H. (1960). *Enjoy, Enjoy*. Cleveland: World.

Hacker, A. (1992). *Two Nations: Black and White, Separate, Hostile, Unequal*. New York: Ballantine.

Hale-Benson, J. (1990) "Visions for Children: Educating Black Children in the Context of their Culture," in *Going to School*.

Hine, L. (1909). "Photography: How the Camera May Help in the Social Uplift." National Conference of Charities and Corrections Proceedings (pp. 355-359).

Huff, A. (1991). *The History of South Carolina in the Building of the Nation*. Greenville, SC: Furman University Press.

Inger, M. (1969). *Politics and Reality in an American City: The New Orleans School Crisis of 1960*. New York: Center for Urban Education.

Innerst, C. "Putting Africa on the Map," *Washington Times*, November 13, 1990.

Jeansonne, G. (1977). *Leander Perez: Boss of the Delta*. Baton Rouge: Louisiana State University Press.

Jencks, C., et al. (1979). *Who Gets Ahead?* New York: Basic.

Jones, L. (1985) *South Carolina: One of the Fifty States*. Orangeburg, SC: Sandlapper Publishing.

Katz, M. (1989). *The Undeserving Poor*. New York: Pantheon.

Kovel, J. (1970). *White Racism: A Psychohistory*. New York: Random House.

Kozol, J. (1991). *Savage Inequalities*. New York: Crown.

Kozol, J. (1987). *Rachel and Her Children*. New York: Crown.

LeClerq, J. "How Far Does Freedom Extend." *The Gamecock*, December 9, 1955, p. 6.

Lemanns, N. (1991). *The Promised Land: The Great Black Migration and How It Changed America*. New York: Knopf.

Leo, J. "A Fringe History of the World," *U.S. News and World Report*, November 12, 1990.

Levinsohn, F. & Wright, B. (1976). *School Integration: Shadow and Substance*. Chicago: University of Chicago Press.

Lochbaum, J. (1993). "The Word Made Flesh: The Desegregation Leadership of the Rev. J. A. DeLaine." unpublished doctoral dissertation, University of South Carolina.

Lomotey, K. (1990). *Going to School: The African-American Experience*. Albany: SUNY Press.

Long, R. (1989). "The African Diaspora," in *Infusion of African and African-American Content in the School Curriculum*.

Louisiana Advisory Committee to the U.S. Civil Rights Commission, Washington, 1961.

Lukas, A. J. (1985). *Common Ground: A Turbulent Decade in the Lives of Three American Families*. New York: Knopf.

Massey, D., & Denton, N. (1993). *American Apartheid: Segregation and the Making of the Underclass*. Cambridge: Harvard University Press.

McCarthy, C. (1990). "Race and Education in the United States: The Multicultural Solution," *Interchange*, v. 21, n. 3, Fall.

McClung, C. "Travelstead Says Board Fired Him," *The Gamecock*, December 2, 1955, pp. 1, 2.

McDonnell, J. "Moist Compassion," *National Review*, December 13, 1985.

Mehl, B. (1974). *Classic Educational Ideas*. Columbus: Merrill.

Mellette, B. "Travelstead—We Are In South Carolina," *The Gamecock*, December 9, 1955, p. 6.

Mills, C. W. (1951). *White Collar*. New York: Oxford University Press.

Mills, C. W. (1959). *The Power Elite*. New York: Oxford University Press.

Muller, M. L. (1975) "The New Orleans Parish School Board and Negro Education," unpublished master's degree thesis, University of New Orleans.

Murray, C. (1984). *Losing Ground*. New York: Basic.

New Orleans Times Picayune, August 31 and November 16, 1960.

Newby, I. A. (1957). "South Carolina and the Desegregation Issue: 1954–1956," unpublished masters thesis, University of South Carolina.

Newby, I. A. (1973). *Black Carolinians: A History of Blacks in South Carolina from 1895 to 1968*. Columbia, SC: University of South Carolina Press.

Newsweek, November 28, 1960.

Oliphant, M. (1932, 1940) *The Simms History of South Carolina*. Columbia, SC: The State Company.

Oliphant, M. (1958,1970). *The History of South Carolina*. River Forest, IL: Laidlaw Brothers.

Ogbu, J. (1978). *Minority Education and Caste*. New York: Academic Press.

"Portland African-American Baseline Essays." Portland, Oregon: Portland Public Schools, 1989.

Puckett, J. R. (1984). *Five Photo-Textual Documentaries from the Great Depression*. Ann Arbor: UMI Research Press.

Riis, J. (1971). *How the Other Half Lives*. New York: Dover.

Roberts, R. "Texan Applauds Trustees," *The Gamecock*, December 2, 1955, p. 2.

Robertson, I. (1977). *Sociology*. New York: Worth.

Robinson, G. "Race and Class," *The Progressive*, March 1986.

Rogers, K.L. (1982). "Hearts and Minds." Unpublished Ph.D dissertation, University of Minnesota. (Rogers published a book on the topic *Righteous Lives: Narratives of the New Orleans Civil Rights Movement*. New York: New York University Press, 1993).

Rosenblum, W., Rosenblum, N., & Trachtenberg, A. (1977). *America and Lewis Hines*. New York: Aperture.

Ryan, W. (1971). *Blaming the Victim*. New York: Random House.

Sharpe, S. G. (1939). *Tobe*. Chapel Hill: University of North Carolina Press.

Schuman, H., Steeh, C., & Bobo, L. (1987). *Racial Attitudes in America*. Cambridge: Harvard University Press.

Simms, W. G. (1917, 1922). *The History of South Carolina*. Columbia, SC: The State Company.

Stott, W. (1973). *Documentary Expression and Thirties America*. New York: Oxford University Press.

Stryker, R. (1973). *In This Proud Land*. Greenwich, CT: New York Graphic Society.

Sullivan, A. "Racism 101," *The New Republic,* November 26, 1990.

Terkel, S. (1992). *Race: How Blacks and Whites Think and Feel About the American Obsession*. New York: New Press.

Timmerman, G. Inaugural address of the honorable George Bell Timmerman, Jr. as Governor of South Carolina, January 18, 1955.

Travelstead, C. (1956). "Turmoil in the Deep South," *School and Society*, 83, 143–147.

Tyack, D., Lowe, R., & Hansot, E. (1984). *Public Schools in Hard Times*. Cambridge: Harvard University Press.

Watkins, C. (1982) "The Blurred Image" (Unpublished dissertation, University of Delaware).

Weber, J. (1891). *Fifty Lessons in the History of South Carolina*. Boston: Ginn and Company.

Weinberg, M. (1981). *The Whites Who Stayed*. Westport, CT: Greenwood Press.

West, C. (1993). *Race Matters*. Boston: Beacon.

White, H. (1906). *The Making of South Carolina*. New York: Silver, Burdett.

Wieder, A. "Modern Education in the United States," *Journal of Thought*, November 1979.

Wieder, A. (1984). "Carpooling for Desegregation," *Integrated Education*.

Wieder, A. (1986). "A Principal and Desegregation," *Equity and Excellence*, Summer.

Wilkins, R. "Not By Bootstraps Alone," *Village Voice*, February 4, 1986.

Wilson, J. Q. "The Judge and the Schools," *Commentary*, January 1986.

Wilson, W. J. (1987) *The Truly Disadvantaged*. Chicago: University of Chicago Press.

Wright, R. (1941). *12 Million Black Voices*. New York: Viking.

Zanger, M. "Crossfire," *The Nation*. October 5, 1985.

COUNTERPOINTS publishes the most compelling and imaginative books being written in education today. Grounded on the theoretical advances in criticalism, feminism and postmodernism in the last two decades of the twentieth century, Counterpoints engages the meaning of these innovations in various forms of educational expression. Committed to the proposition that theoretical literature should be accessible to a variety of audiences, the series insists that its authors avoid esoteric and jargonistic languages that transform educational scholarship into an elite discourse for the initiated. Scholarly work matters only to the degree it affects consciousness and practice at multiple sites. Counterpoints' editorial policy is based on these principles and the ability of scholars to break new ground, to open new conversations, to go where educators have never gone before.